JONATHAN EDWARDS AND THE ENLIGHTENMENT

Problems in American Civilization

JONATHAN EDWARDS AND THE ENLIGHTENMENT

Edited with an Introduction by

John Opie

DUQUESNE UNIVERSITY

D. C. HEATH AND COMPANY
A Division of Raytheon Education Company
Lexington, Massachusetts

INTRODUCTION

WILLIAM HAZLITT, the perceptive and widely-read eighteenth-century English essayist, insisted that there were only six philosophers of any value in his day. He listed them as Hobbes, Berkeley, Butler, Hartley, Hume and Leibniz. But he felt compelled to add a seventh to this select group, "a Massachusetts man," Jonathan Edwards. Hazlitt's judgment was not a solitary one. Although Edwards lived out his days in seeming geographical and intellectual isolation, at the wilderness pulpit of Northampton in western Massachusetts and at the primitive Indian mission at Stockbridge, his works were widely published in the English-speaking world and repeatedly translated and printed in Europe. His correspondence includes exchanges with some of the best minds of England and Scotland. Just as he was surprisingly up to date concerning the intellectual currents of the Age of Reason, so his own writings were speedily printed in more civilized regions.

Despite Hazlitt's praise, today Jonathan Edwards is largely remembered as a violent and sarcastic preacher of the immediacy of hell-fire in the turbulent Great Awakening in the 1740's. This memory makes him the practitioner of an exotic profession which most modern readers conclude has lost its significance for American life. In his own day Edwards was looked upon as an outdated but troublesome revivalist by his supposedly more enlightened contemporaries. Until recently, twentieth-century intellectuals, like their Enlightenment predecessors, had concluded that the eighteenth century was a century when exceedingly repressive Puritan doctrines that had hobbled man's natural capacities were being rapidly and properly eclipsed by the appealing optimistic faith of the Age of Reason. Edwards, it appeared, was left far behind by a climate of opinion which cooled the fires of hell and brought on the colonial revolution and American independence.

However, with the possible exception of Benjamin Franklin, Edwards was the most influential and widely-read writer of colonial America. Despite his premature death at fifty-four, the relatively small body of writings published in his own lifetime, and his seemingly narrow preoccupation with the dangers of free-will Arminianism and the potential of religious revivals, new editions of his works rapidly followed one another until well into the nineteenth century. A newly edited complete edition is even under way today.

If Edwards appeared singularly out-of-season in his own day and even more so for succeeding generations, why were his sermons, tracts and books so widely read, debated and reprinted for another century? Further, why has Edwards invariably stimulated modern students of the American mind not only to reading him day and night, but to spread widely different interpretations of his contribution to American life? Edwards has an intellectual and spiritual elusiveness which does not allow the reader to pour him into any pre-cast mold.

Whatever conclusions the reader may reach about the real Edwards, he was the most acute American analyst of the achievements of the Enlightenment, far surpassing the perceptiveness of Franklin, Mayhew, Paine, and even Jefferson, in science, psychology, and philosophy. As a New England divine, Edwards was one of the rare breed anywhere to recognize and accept the direct challenge given traditional Christianity by the physical discoveries of Newton, the psychological observations of Locke, and the popular acceptance of a "God more kind and man more worthy." He attempted to join these divergent movements together with a surprisingly bold use of the Bible as revelation. He admitted that many orthodox beliefs concerning man's "understanding" and "affections" had been inadequately explained. Yet he refused to exchange his strenuous Puritan theology for the prevailing enlightened morality. Edwards clearly joined a select circle of eighteenth-century intellectuals who recognized that the struggle for the contemporary mind would not result in a decisive victory for the widely lauded physical scientists nor for those who claimed privy to the councils of heaven. Ultimately philosophical controversies of the Enlightenment did not focus their attention on metaphysics, but turned to questions of epistemology which remain the preoccupation of modern philosophy. The struggles of the Enlightenment would be won by the person or persons who produced a revolutionary theory of the workings of the human mind which would be scientifically demonstrable, logically sound, and intellectually comprehensive.

Edwards' intellectual life began after the English Enlightenment had already reached its maturity. The new worlds of matter and spirit proposed by Descartes, Newton, and Locke had already conquered the western mind. Arriving in 1716 at the fledgling and strife-torn Connecticut Collegiate School, later Yale College, Edwards had the good fortune to benefit from Jeremy Dummer's handsome gift of books the previous year. His college curriculum was a mixed bag, including traditional topics like scholastic logic, the Bible in Greek and Hebrew, and the Puritan patriarch William Ames. But also at hand were Locke, Newton and even popular Cartesianism through the works of the Port Royal logicians, Antoine Arnauld and Pierre Nicolet. Edwards was encouraged to probe this revolutionary thought as well as the traditional divines.

The contribution and controversy of Jonathan Edwards can be summed up in the words "experimental religion." He was inevitably religious because his public life and the life of his mind were cast in an orthodox New England Puritan mold. He was simultaneously experimental because he seized for his own use the new science and psychology of Newton and Locke. Caught up in the enthusiasm of the revivals while deeply disturbed by contemporary tendencies to blur the harsh reality of God, he probed with unparalleled clarity and rare precision the intellectual crises of his generation. He was truly "the Puritan in the Age of Reason." Edwards concluded that his generation abounded with false conceptions of the nature of man, and devoted himself to an analysis of the means by which man acquired knowledge, of what caused him to will good and evil, and of what gave him intense emotions, either with integrity or through "overheated imaginations." His thought and actions always rested directly on the Christian traditions of original sin and irresistible grace, but he also believed with the most sophisticated exponents of the new empirical science that all knowledge was based upon sense experience. Edwards' realization of the intellectual and spiritual crisis which the Enlightenment brought to western man was singularly intensified by the Great Awakening, to which he was drawn like a magnet. He came to believe in earnest that the revivals, whatever their excesses, were

observable phenomena and therefore ir-
refutable manifestations of the reality of
supernatural intervention in human affairs. Edwards' loyalty to matters of religion in a passionately anti-clerical age
brought him anguish, and derision, and
cast doubts upon his intellectual integrity
even while men admired his insights.
Few contemporaries had the breadth of
insight to comprehend the meaning of
his claims. Rather, theologians attacked
him for his apparent defense of an orgy
of the emotions, while the new rationalists despised him for his continued
support of outdated Puritan beliefs.

Edwards gladly accepted the pulpit as
his stage and theology as his natural
idiom of thought; he never conceived of
any other activity for himself. Primarily
a sermon writer, his manuscripts included 1074 sermon booklets, of which
568 still exist. Within the scope of his
religious activities, he was one of those
rare persons who founded an original
system of thought which raced far beyond his rationalist contemporaries, and
who also directed a popular movement,
the Great Awakening, which itself became the standard by which all American religious revivals have been tested.
These very different activities which
alone have made Edwards worthy of
consideration, have also created the controversy which surrounds him. At the
same time that his *Religious Affections*
and *Inquiry into Free Will* were gaining
him fame in England and Europe for
their intellectual accomplishments, he
came under colonial suspicion for anti-
intellectualism. Did he restore Puritan
strenuousness after an era in which religion declined from the mythological
greatness of the founders of Massachusetts Bay, or did he submit religion to
the corrosive effects of intense emotion-
alism? "Our people," he once wrote, "do
not so much need to have their heads

stored, as to have their hearts touched."

Or to avoid a misleading polarization
between enthusiast and rationalist, did
Edwards' religious idiom hide "the first
great American scientist, psychologist
and philosopher?" Because of the dated
outlook of Puritan theology even in Edwards' day, and because of modern man's
distrust of religious authoritarianism, this
concept of a secular thinker hidden behind a theological cloak has considerable
modern appeal. If Edwards had not
burned himself out on the Great Awakening and his massive refutation of
Arminianism, are there signs he might
have gone far in a remarkable secular
direction of his own? This possibility
turns his early death from smallpox contracted by voluntary innoculation into an
ironic tragedy. Further, his later philosophical notes and writings deal more
with the preoccupation with morality,
conscience, and virtue characteristic of
the Age of Reason, and less with the
bitter theological controversies over revivalism and Arminianism. Does his
mental activity bear a strange resemblance to that of his erstwhile rationalist
critics? Or stranger yet, if the theology
can be wiped clean off our reading of his
works, do we find ourselves in the company of the transcendentalism of Emerson, the idealism of Josiah Royce, the
pragmatism of William James and even
some significant anticipations of modern
psychoanalytical thought?

The first section of the text will allow
the reader to explore the effect of the
Enlightenment upon this Massachusetts
clergyman. Since Edwards' connections
with Locke, or the lack of them, are the
key to the controversy, selections from
Locke's *Essay Concerning Human Understanding* are paralleled with relevant
excerpts from Edwards' youthful and
mature writings. Next, Perry Miller
argues that Edwards' use of Locke al-

lowed him insights into the significance of the Enlightenment that far surpassed his supposedly more liberal contemporaries. Miller's modernizing, however, comes under trenchant attack in Vincent Tomas's critical review. Tomas believes Edwards remained a medieval because of his unyielding biblical orientation. Edwards' youthful and sophisticated use of Newton has also intrigued modern interpreters. A brief selection from Edwards on optics is followed by Clarence Faust's misgivings about Edwards' scientific capacity and Theodore Hornberger's direct rebuttal of Faust by noting Edwards' appropriation of Newtonian physics throughout his writings.

The second set of readings is devoted to Edwards' participation in the philosophical and theological debates which preoccupied his contemporaries on both sides of the Atlantic. Although the specific form of controversy dates these selections, the questions raised are surprisingly modern. The reader has the opportunity to consider how broadly and deeply Edwards was involved. The widely-influential Anglican divine John Taylor, sometimes called "the father of English Arminianism," decries orthodox views of human sin and depravity as morally and intellectually inhibiting, while Edwards replies directly to Taylor by noting the deleterious effects of such liberalism. Edwards found much of value in Francis Hutcheson's views on morality, but believed that Hutcheson had only begun to probe the intricacies of virtue, beauty and truth. Finally, Edwards' involvement in the noisy and pietistic Great Awakening led to his careful synthesis of reason and "affections" which merged elements of Puritan and Enlightenment thought.

The selections conclude with a series of readings drawn from diverse twen-tieth-century interpreters. Vernon Parrington defends the long-standing and widely-held position that Edwards' narrow and strict Puritanism was badly suited to the emerging liberal modernity of eighteenth-century America. Ola Winslow finds more modernity in Edwards' youthful development but suggests that the Great Awakening and the threat of Arminianism tragically drew all of Edwards' energies and prevented him from ever developing his early "enlightened" thoughts. Peter Gay, drawing upon his background as historian of the European Enlightenment, indicates that Perry Miller and other champions of the greatness and modernity of Edwards have overstated their case. Like Winslow, Gay believes there were impediments in Edwards' thought and development which he did not conquer. Finally, Conrad Cherry's recent and balanced study attempts to take many diverse elements in Edwards' own thought, to make careful use of other interpreters' insights, and outline the diverse and complex character of Edwards' intellectual life.

Edwards' thought and controversialism caused his interpreters to clash for over 200 years. Today many of the specific religious questions he wrestled with have little relevance to most Americans. But few can deny his logical clarity, his penetration of universal philosophical, psychological and religious issues, and his expanded vision which sought to comprehend in one mind the awesome Puritan God with a new empirical and moralistic humanitarianism. The historian Bancroft a century ago wrote, "He that would know the workings of the New England mind in the middle of the last century, and the throbbings of its heart, must give his days and nights to the study of Jonathan Edwards."

CONTENTS

Important Dates

1630   Massachusetts Bay Colony founded.

1672   Isaac Newton's letter to the Royal Society, "New Theory about Light and Colors."

1686   Isaac Newton, *Principia.*

1690   John Locke, *Essay Concerning Human Understanding.*

1703   Jonathan Edwards born at East Windsor, Connecticut, on October 5.

1715   Wrote "Of Insects."

1716–1722 Studied at Yale College, four years undergraduate, two years theology. Read Newton and Locke. Wrote "Notes on Mind," and "Notes on Natural Science." Conversion experience.

1724–1726 Tutor at Yale.

1725   Francis Hutcheson, *An Inquiry into the Original of Our Ideas of Beauty and Virtue.*

1727   Assistant minister at Northampton, Massachusetts, where his grandfather, Solomon Stoddard, was minister until his death in 1729. Edwards then became sole minister.

1731   First publication: *God Glorified in Man's Dependence,* the Boston Election sermon.

1734–1737 First Northampton revival. *A Faithful Narrative of the Surprising Work of God in the Conversion of Many Hundred Souls.*

1738   Samuel Clarke, *Discourse concerning the Being and Attributes of God.*

1740   John Taylor, *The Scripture-Doctrine of Original Sin.*

1740–1742 The Great Awakening in New England.

1741   Sermon at Enfield, Connecticut, *Sinners in the Hands of an Angry God.*

1743   Charles Chauncy, *Seasonable Thoughts on the State of Religion in New England.*

1746   *A Treatise Concerning Religious Affections,* preached 1742–1743.

1751   Settled in Stockbridge, Massachusetts, frontier mission, after dissensions in Northampton.

1754   *A Careful and Strict Enquiry into the Modern Prevailing Notions of that Freedom of Will.*

1755   Wrote *The Nature of True Virtue* and *Concerning the End for which God Created the World,* published posthumously in 1765 as *Two Dissertations.*

1757   Named president of the College of New Jersey (now Princeton).

1758   *The Great Christian Doctrine of Original Sin Defended.* Died from aftereffects of smallpox vaccination on March 22.

The Clash of Issues

Edwards speaks from an insight into science and psychology so much ahead of his time that our own can hardly be said to have caught up with him.

Perry Miller

Far from being the first modern American, he was the last medieval American.

Peter Gay

By rejecting the possibility of innate ideas in man's mind, John Locke played a major role in revolutionizing the western intellectual tradition:

Let us suppose the mind to be white paper, void of all characters, without any ideas: — How comes it to be furnished? Whence comes it by that vast store which the busy and boundless fancy of man has appointed on it with an almost endless variety? Whence has it all the *materials* of reason and knowledge? To this I answer, in one word, from EXPERIENCE. In that all our knowledge is founded.

A modern historian suggests that in colonial America Edwards alone not only understood Locke's accomplishment, but went far beyond it:

The boy of fourteen grasped in a flash . . . that Locke was the master-spirit of the age, and that the *Essay* made everything then being offered at Harvard or Yale as philosophy, psychology and rhetoric so obsolete that it could no longer be taken seriously. . . . When Edwards stood up among the New England clergy, it was as though a master of relativity spoke to a convention of Newtonians who had not yet heard of Einstein, or as though among nineteenth-century professors of psychology, all assuming that man is rational and responsible, a strange youth began to refer, without more ado, to the id, ego, and super-ego.

Perry Miller

An English "Arminian" sought to liberalize Christian theology, and found Calvinistic original sin both morally unquestionable and unreasonable:

What can be more destructive of virtue than to have a notion that you must, in some degree or other, be necessarily vicious? And hath not the common doctrine of original sin a manifest tendency to propagate such a notion? . . . . For to represent sin as natural, as altogether unavoidable, is to embolden in sin, and to give not only an excuse, but a reason for sinning. . . . Such doctrines set religion in direct opposition to reason and common sense, and so render our rational powers quite useless to us, and consequently religion too. For a religion which we cannot understand, or which is not the object of a rational belief, is no religion for reasonable beings.

John Taylor

On the other hand, Edwards sought to establish a synthesis of Puritanism and Enlightenment thought by which he could defend traditional doctrines like original sin:

This depravity is both odious, and also pernicious, fatal and destructive, in the highest sense, as inevitably tending to that which implies man's eternal ruin; it shows that man, as he is by nature, is in a deplorable and undone state. . . . [therefore] It is wholly impertinent to talk of the innocent and kind actions, even of criminals themselves, surpassing their crimes in numbers, and of the prevailing innocence, good nature, industry, felicity, and cheerfulness of the greater part of mankind.

Edwards' defense of Puritan orthodoxy led one historian to suggest that he was badly outdated even in the eighteenth century:

In the midst of the greatest revolution in the European mind since Christianity had overwhelmed paganism, Edwards serenely reaffirmed the faith of his fathers. . . . The physical universe of Edwards was not the physical universe of Newton: it was a universe created in six days, filled with angels and devils, with a heaven and hell, a universe in the hands, and at the mercy, of an angry God.

PETER GAY

Still another historian argues that Edwards was neither medieval nor modern, but a man involved in the problems of his own era:

The interests which occupied Edwards' chief attention were theological — interests which increasingly had their immediate occasions in the theological issues facing eighteenth-century New England.

CONRAD CHERRY

I. THE INFLUENCE OF JOHN LOCKE
UPON EDWARDS

John Locke: NEW THEORY OF KNOWLEDGE

John Locke (1632–1704) dominated philosophical developments in the English Enlightenment as did no other man. Combining the rationalism of René Descartes and the empiricism of Isaac Newton, he attacked the prevailing conception of "innate ideas" in his famous Essay concerning Human Understanding *(1690). In a short time Locke's theory revolutionized speculations about how man thinks and acquires knowledge. Ever since, modern philosophy has been preoccupied with epistemology and psychology rather than metaphysics. Set forth in this selection is his central argument that the human mind is a blank tablet (tabula rasa) until through the senses it experiences the external world and the internal operations of the mind. What is received through sense experience are irreducible and reliable "ideas," simply and directly acquired, and these become more complex by means of reflective operations within the mind. The selection concludes with Locke's important description of how personal continuity or identity is preserved in his theory.*

LET US THEN suppose the mind to be, as we say, white paper, void of all characters, without any ideas: — How comes it to be furnished? Whence comes it by that vast store which the busy and boundless fancy of man has painted on it with an almost endless variety? Whence has it all the *materials* of reason and knowledge? To this I answer, in one word, from EXPERIENCE. In that all our knowledge is founded; and from that it ultimately derives itself. Our observation employed either, about external sensible objects, or about the internal operations of our minds perceived and reflected on by ourselves, is that which supplies our understandings with all the *materials* of thinking. These two are the fountains of knowledge, from whence all the ideas we

have, or can naturally have, do spring.

First, our Senses, conversant about particular sensible objects, do convey into the mind several distinct perceptions of things, according to those various ways wherein those objects do affect them. And thus we come by those *ideas* we have of *yellow, white, heat, cold, soft, hard, bitter, sweet,* and all those which we call sensible qualities; which when I say the senses convey into the mind, I mean, they from external objects convey into the mind what produces there those perceptions. This great source of most of the ideas we have, depending wholly upon our senses, and derived by them to the understanding, I call SENSATION.

Secondly, the other fountain from which experience furnisheth the under-

From John Locke, *An Essay concerning Human Understanding*, 2 vols., ed. by Alexander Campbell Fraser (Oxford: Oxford University Press, 1894), vol. I, pp. 121–126, 213–217, 458–461.

standing with ideas is, — the perception of the operations of our own mind within us, as it is employed about the ideas it has got; — which operations, when the soul comes to reflect on and consider, do furnish the understanding with another set of ideas, which could not be had from things without. And such are *perception, thinking, doubting, believing, reasoning, knowing, willing,* and all the different actings of our own minds; — which we being conscious of, and observing in ourselves, do from these receive into our understandings as distinct ideas as we do from bodies affecting our senses. This source of ideas every man has wholly in himself; and though it be not sense, as having nothing to do with external objects, yet it is very like it, and might properly enough be called *internal sense.* But as I call the other Sensation, so I call this REFLECTION, the ideas it affords being such only as the mind gets by reflecting on its own operations within itself. By reflection then, in the following part of this discourse, I would be understood to mean, that notice which the mind takes of its own operations, and the manner of them, by reason whereof there come to be ideas of these operations in the understanding. These two, I say, viz. external material things, as the objects of SENSATION, and the operations of our own minds within, as the objects of REFLECTION, are to me the only originals from whence all our ideas take their beginnings. The term *operations* here I use in a large sense, as comprehending not barely the actions of the mind about its ideas, but some sort of passions arising sometimes from them, such as is the satisfaction or uneasiness arising from any thought.

The understanding seems to me not to have the least glimmering of any ideas which it doth not receive from one of these two. *External objects* furnish the mind with the ideas of sensible qualities, which are all those different perceptions they produce in us; and *the mind* furnishes the understanding with ideas of its own operations.

These, when we have taken a full survey of them, and their several modes, [combinations, and relations,] we shall find to contain all our whole stock of ideas; and that we have nothing in our minds which did not come in one of these two ways. Let any one examine his own thoughts, and thoroughly search into his understanding; and then let him tell me, whether all the original ideas he has there, are any other than of the objects of his senses, or of the operations of his mind, considered as objects of his reflection. And how great a mass of knowledge soever he imagines to be lodged there, he will, upon taking a strict view, see that he has not any idea in his mind but what one of these two have imprinted; — though perhaps, with infinite variety compounded and enlarged by the understanding, as we shall see hereafter.

He that attentively considers the state of a child, at his first coming into the world, will have little reason to think him stored with plenty of ideas, that are to be the matter of his future knowledge. It is *by degrees* he comes to be furnished with them. And though the ideas of obvious and familiar qualities imprint themselves before the memory begins to keep a register of time or order, yet it is often so late before some unusual qualities come in the way, that there are few men that cannot recollect the beginning of their acquaintance with them. And if it were worth while, no doubt a child might be so ordered as to have but a very few, even of the ordinary ideas, till he were grown up to a man. But all that are born into the world, being surrounded with bodies that perpetually and diversely affect them, variety of ideas, whether care be taken of it or not, are imprinted on the minds of children. Light and colours are busy at hand everywhere, when the eye is but open; sounds and some tangible qualities fail not to solicit their proper senses, and force an entrance to the mind; — but yet, I think, it will be granted easily, that if a child were kept in a place where he never saw any other but black and white till he were a man, he would have no more ideas of scarlet or green, than he that from his childhood never tasted an oyster, or a pine-apple, has of those particular relishes.

* * *

We have hitherto considered those ideas, in the reception whereof the mind is only passive, which are those simple ones received from sensation and reflection before mentioned, whereof the mind cannot make one to itself, nor have any idea which does not wholly consist of them. [But as the mind is wholly passive in the reception of all its simple ideas, so it exerts several acts of its own, whereby out of its simple ideas, as the materials and foundations of the rest, the others are framed. The acts of the mind, wherein it exerts its power over its simple ideas, are chiefly these three: (1) Combining several simple ideas into one compound one; and thus all *complex ideas* are made. (2) The second is bringing two ideas, whether simple or complex, together, and setting them by one another, so as to take a view of them at once, without uniting them into one; by which way it gets all its *ideas of relations.* (3) The third is separating them from all other ideas that accompany

them in their real existence: this is called abstraction: and thus all its *general ideas* are made. This shows man's power, and its ways of operation, to be much the same in the material and intellectual world. For the materials in both being such as he has no power over, either to make or destroy, all that man can do is either to unite them together, or to set them by one another, or wholly separate them. I shall here begin with the first of these in the consideration of complex ideas, and come to the other two in their due places.] As simple ideas are observed to exist in several combinations united together, so the mind has a power to consider several of them united together as one idea; and that not only as they are united in external objects, but as itself has joined them together. Ideas thus made up of several simple ones put together, I call *complex;* — such as are beauty, gratitude, a man, an army, the universe; which, though complicated of various simple ideas, or complex ideas made up of simple ones, yet are, when the mind pleases, considered each by itself, as one entire thing, and signified by one name.

In this faculty of repeating and joining together its ideas, the mind has great power in varying and multiplying the objects of its thoughts, infinitely beyond what sensation or reflection furnished it with: but all this still confined to those simple ideas which it received from those two sources, and which are the ultimate materials of all its compositions. For simple ideas are all from things themselves, and of these the mind *can* have no more, nor other than what are suggested to it. It can have no other ideas of sensible qualities than what come from without by the senses; nor any ideas of other kind of operations of a thinking substance, than what it finds in itself.

But when it has once got these simple ideas, it is not confined barely to observation, and what offers itself from without; it can, by its own power, put together those ideas it has, and make new complex ones, which it never received so united.

Complex ideas, however compounded and decompounded, though their number be infinite, and the variety endless, wherewith they fill and entertain the thoughts of men; yet I think they may be all reduced under these three heads: —

1. MODES.
2. SUBSTANCES.
3. RELATIONS.

First, *Modes* I call such complex ideas which, however compounded, contain not in them the supposition of subsisting by themselves, but are considered as dependences on, or affections of substances; — such as are the ideas signified by the words triangle, gratitude, murder, &c. And if in this I use the word mode in somewhat a different sense from its ordinary signification, I beg pardon; it being unavoidable in discourses, differing from the ordinary received notions, either to make new words, or to use old words in somewhat a new signification; the later whereof, in our present case, is perhaps the more tolerable of the two.

Of these *modes,* there are two sorts which deserve distinct consideration: —

First, there are some which are only variations, or different combinations of the same simple idea, without the mixture of any other; — as a dozen, or score; which are nothing but the ideas of so many distinct units added together, and these I call *simple modes* as being contained within the bounds of one simple idea.

Secondly, there are others compounded of simple ideas of several kinds, put together to make one complex one; — v.g. beauty, consisting of a certain composition of colour and figure, causing delight to the beholder; theft, which being the concealed change of the possession of anything, without the consent of the proprietor, contains, as is visible, a combination of several ideas of several kinds: and these I call *mixed modes.*

Secondly, the ideas of *substances* are such combinations of simple ideas as are taken to represent distinct *particular* things subsisting by themselves; in which the supposed or confused idea of substance, such as it is, is always the first and chief. Thus if to substance be joined the simple idea of a certain dull whitish colour, with certain degrees of weight, hardness, ductility, and fusibility, we have the idea of lead; and a combination of the ideas of a certain sort of figure, with the powers of motion, thought and reasoning, joined to substance, make the ordinary idea of a man. Now of substances also, there are two sorts of ideas: — one of *single* substances, as they exist separately, as of a man or a sheep; the other of several of those put together, as an army of men, or flock of sheep — which *collective* ideas of several substances thus put together are as much each of them one single idea as that of a man or an unit.

Thirdly, the last sort of complex ideas is that we call *relation,* which consists in the consideration and comparing one idea with another. . . .

If we trace the progress of our minds, and with attention observe how it repeats, adds together, and unites its simple ideas received from sensation or reflection, it will lead us further than at first perhaps we should have imagined. And, I believe, we shall find, if we warily observe the originals of our notions, that *even the most abstruse ideas,* how remote soever they may seem from sense, or from any operations of our own minds, are yet only such as the understanding frames to itself, by repeating and joining together ideas that it had either from objects of sense, or from its own operations about them: so that those even large and abstract ideas are derived from sensation or reflection, being no other than what the mind, by the ordinary use of its own faculties, employed about ideas received from objects of sense, or from the operations it observes in itself about them, may, and does, attain unto.

* * *

It is plain, consciousness, as far as ever it can be extended — should it be to ages past — unites existences and actions very remote in time into the same *person,* as well as it does the existences and actions of the immediately preceding moment: so that whatever has the consciousness of present and past actions, is the same person to whom they both belong. Had I the same consciousness that I saw the ark and Noah's flood, as that I saw an overflowing of the Thames last winter, or as that I write now, I could no more doubt that I who write this now, that saw the Thames overflowed last winter, and that viewed the flood at the general deluge, was the same *self,* — place that self in what *substance* you please — than that I who write this am the same *myself* now whilst I write (whether I consist of all the same substance, material or immaterial, or no) that I was yesterday. For as to this point of being the same self, it matters not whether this present self be made up of the same or other substances — I being as much concerned, and as justly accountable for any action that was done a thousand years since, appropriated to me now by this self-consciousness, as I am for what I did the last moment.

Self is that conscious thinking thing, — whatever substance made up of, (whether spiritual or material, simple or compounded, it matters not) — which is sensible or conscious of pleasure and pain, capable of happiness or misery, and so is concerned for itself, as far as that consciousness extends. Thus every one finds that, whilst comprehended under that consciousness, the little finger is as much a part of himself as what is most so. Upon separation of this little finger, should this consciousness go along with the little finger, and leave the rest of the body, it is evident the little finger would be the person, the same person; and self then would have nothing to do with the rest of the body. As in this case it is the consciousness that goes along with the substance, when one part is separate from another, which makes the same person, and constitutes this inseparable self: so it is in reference to substances remote in time. That with which the consciousness of this present thinking thing *can* join itself, makes the same person, and is one self with it, and with nothing else; and so attributes to itself, and owns all the actions of that thing, as its own, as far as that consciousness reaches, and no further; as every one who reflects will perceive.

In this personal identity is founded all the right and justice of reward and punishment; happiness and misery being that for which every one is concerned for *himself,* and not mattering what becomes of any *substance,* not joined to, or affected with that consciousness. For, as it is evident in the instance I gave but now, if the consciousness went along with the little finger when it was cut off, that would be the same self which was concerned for the whole body yesterday, as making part of itself, whose actions then it cannot but admit as its own now.

Though, if the same body should still live, and immediately from the separation of the little finger have its own peculiar consciousness, whereof the little finger knew nothing, it would not at all be concerned for it, as a part of itself, or could own any of its actions, or have any of them imputed to him.

This may show us wherein personal identity consists: not in the identity of substance, but, as I have said, in the identity of consciousness, wherein if Socrates and the present mayor of Queinborough agree, they are the same person: if the same Socrates waking and sleeping does not partake of the same consciousness, Socrates waking and sleeping is not the same person. And to punish Socrates waking for what sleeping Socrates thought, and waking Socrates was never conscious of, would be no more of right, than to punish one twin for what his brother-twin did, whereof he knew nothing, because their outsides were so like, that they could not be distinguished; for such twins have been seen.

But yet possibly it will still be objected, — Suppose I wholly lose the memory of some parts of my life, beyond a possibility of retrieving them, so that perhaps I shall never be conscious of them again; yet am I not the same person that did those actions, had those thoughts that I once was conscious of, though I have now forgot them? To which I answer, that we must here take notice what the word *I* is applied to; which, in this case, is the *man* only. And the same man being presumed to be the same person, I is easily here supposed to stand also for the same person. But if it be possible for the same man to have distinct incommunicable consciousness at different times, it is past doubt the same man would at different times make different persons; which, we see, is the sense of mankind in the solemnest declaration of their opinions, human laws not punishing the mad man for the sober man's actions, nor the sober man for what the mad man did, — thereby making them two persons: which is somewhat explained by our way of speaking in English when we say such an one is "not himself," or is "beside himself"; in which phrases it is insinuated, as if those who now, or at least first used them, thought that self was changed; the self-same person was no longer in that man.

Jonathan Edwards: YOUNG FOLLOWER OF LOCKE

Philosophers and historians have been drawn to Jonathan Edwards' notes entitled "The Mind" which Edwards composed while a youthful student at Yale, when he was either fourteen in 1717, or sixteen in 1719. Their precocious originality parallels Bishop George Berkeley's philosophical idealism written in England at about the same time, but apparently unknown to Edwards. At Yale, reading inside the classroom included Tully and Virgil, the logic of Peter Ramus, Francis Bergers-

From Sereno E. Dwight, *The Life of President Edwards* (New York: G. and C. and H. Carvill, 1830), pp. 680–681, 683, 687–688, 690–691, 701.

dicius and Adrian Heereboord, as well as Greek and Hebrew and William Ames's Medulla. Debate has arisen, therefore, concerning the possibility of Edwards' dependence upon Locke's Essay, which was not in the curriculum and quite a rare book in the colonies. Yet, Samuel Hopkins, Edwards' devoted disciple and first biographer, wrote that Edwards told him personally that in his youth at college "he was much engaged and had more satisfaction and pleasure in studying it, 'than the most greedy miser in gathering handfuls of silver and gold from some newly discovered treasure.'" To a certain extent, Edwards used a Lockean terminology to describe his belief in the ultimate spirituality of the human mind. But perhaps the greater debate is not whether Edwards used Locke, but whether or not other foundations for his thought, such as Puritanism or the Cambridge Platonists, had as controlling an interest over his development.

CONSCIOUSNESS is the mind's perceiving what is in itself — ideas, actions, passions, and everything that is there perceptible. It is a sort of feeling within itself. The mind feels when it thinks, so it feels when it discerns, feels when it loves, and feels when it hates. . . .

Identity of person is what seems never yet to have been explained. It is a mistake that it consists in sameness or identity of consciousness — if by sameness of consciousness be meant having the same ideas hereafter that I have now, with a notion or apprehension that I had had them before, just in the same manner as I now have the same ideas that I had in time past by memory. It is possible, without doubt, in the nature of things for God to annihilate me and after my annihilation to create another being that shall have the same ideas in his mind that I have, and with the like apprehension that he had had them before, in like manner as a person has by memory, and yet I be in no way concerned in it, having no reason to fear what that being shall suffer or to hope for what he shall enjoy. Can anyone deny that it is possible after my annihilation to create two beings in the universe, both of them having my

ideas communicated to them, with such a notion of their having had them before (after the manner of memory) and yet be ignorant one of another? And in such a case will anyone say that both these are one and the same person, as they must be if they are both the same person with me? It is possible there may be two such beings, each having all the ideas that are now in my mind in the same manner that I should have by memory if my own being were continued, and yet these two beings not only be ignorant one of another but also be in a very different state: one in a state of enjoyment and pleasure, and the other in a state of great suffering and torment. Yea, there seems to be nothing of impossibility in the nature of things but that the Most High could, if He saw fit, cause there to be another being who should begin to exist in some distant part of the universe, with the same ideas I now have after the manner of memory, and should henceforward co-exist with me (we both retaining a consciousness of what was before the moment of his first existence in like manner) but thenceforward should have a different train of ideas. Will anyone say that he, in such a case, is the same person with me when I know nothing of his suffering and am never the better for his joys?

*   *   *

Love is not properly said to be an idea any more than understanding is said to be an idea. Understanding and loving are different acts of the mind entirely. And so pleasure and pain are not properly ideas, though pleasure and pain may imply perception in their nature; yet it does not follow that they are properly ideas. There is an act of the mind in it. An idea is only a perception wherein the mind is passive or, rather, subjective. The acts of the mind are not merely ideas. All acts of the mind about its ideas are not themselves mere ideas. Pleasure and pain have their seat in the will and not in the understanding. The will, choice, etc., is nothing else but the mind's being pleased with an idea, or having a superior pleasedness in something thought of, or a desire of a future thing, or a pleasedness in the thought of our union with the thing, or a pleasedness in such a state of ourselves and a degree of pain while we are not in that state, or a disagreeable conception of the contrary state at that time when we desire it.

*   *   *

Sensation. Our senses when sound and in ordinary circumstances are not properly fallible in anything — that is, [if] we mean our experience by our senses. If we mean anything else, neither fallibility nor certainty in any way belongs to the senses. Nor are our senses certain in anything at all any other way than by constant experience by our senses — that is, when our senses make such or such representations we constantly experience that things are in themselves thus or thus. So, when a thing appears after such a manner, I judge it to be at least two rods off, at least two feet broad, but I only know by constant experience that a thing that makes such a representation is so far off and so big. And so my senses are as certain in everything, when I have equal opportunity and occasion to experience. And our senses are said to deceive us in some things because our situation does not allow us to make trial, or our circumstances do not lead us to it, and so we are apt to judge by our experience in other and different cases. Thus, our senses make us think that the moon is among the clouds because we cannot try it so quick, easily, and frequently as we do the distance of things that are nearer. But the senses of an astronomer who observes the parallax of the moon do not deceive him but lead him to the truth. (Though the idea of the moon's distance will never be exercised so quick and naturally upon every occasion, because of the tediousness and infrequency of the trial; and there are not so many ways of trial, so many differences in the moon's appearance from what a lesser thing amongst the clouds would have, as there are in things nearer.) I can remember when I was so young that, seeing two things in the same building, one of which was twice so far off as the other, yet, seeing one over the other, I thought they had been of the same distance, one right over the other. My senses then were deceitful in that thing though they made the same representations as now, and yet now they are not deceitful. The only difference is in experience. Indeed, in some things our senses make no difference in the representation where there is a difference in the things, but in those things our experience by our senses will not lead us to judge at all, and so they will deceive. We are in danger of being deceived by our senses in judging of appearances by our experience in different things, or by judging where we have had no experience, or the like. . . .

Truth. After all that has been said and done, the only adequate definition of truth is the agreement of our ideas with existence. To explain what this existence is, is another thing. In abstract ideas it is nothing but the ideas themselves; so their truth is their consistency with themselves. In things that are supposed to be without us, it is the determination and fixed mode of God's exciting ideas in us. So that truth in these things is an agreement of our ideas with that series in God. It is existence and that is all that we can say. It is impossible that we should explain a perfectly abstract and mere idea of existence; only we always find this, by running of it up, that God and real existence are the same.

Corollary. Hence we learn how properly it may be said that God is and that there is none else. And how proper are these names of the deity, Jehovah, and I am that I am!

Truth is the perception of the relations there are between ideas. Falsehood is the supposition of relations between ideas that are inconsistent with those ideas themselves, not their disagreement with things without. All truth is in the mind, and only there. It is ideas, or what is in the mind alone, that can be the object of the mind. And what we call truth is a consistent supposition of relations between what is the object of the mind. Falsehood is an inconsistent supposition of relations. The truth that is in a mind must be in that mind as to its object and everything pertaining to it. The only foundation of error is inadequateness and imperfection of ideas; for

if the idea were perfect it would be impossible but that all its relations should be perfectly perceived. . . .

Truth, in the general, may be defined after the most strict and metaphysical manner: the consistency and agreement of our ideas with the ideas of God. I confess this, in ordinary conversation, would not half so much tend to enlighten one in the meaning of the word as to say: the agreement of our ideas with the things as they are. But it should be enquired, What is it for our ideas to agree with things as they are — seeing that corporeal things exist no otherwise than mentally, and, as for most other things, they are only abstract ideas? Truth as to external things is the consistency of our ideas with those ideas or that train and series of ideas that are raised in our minds according to God's stated order and law. Truth as to abstract ideas is the consistency of our ideas with themselves — as when our idea of a circle, or a triangle, or any of their parts, is agreeable to the idea we have stated and agreed to call by the name of a circle, or a triangle. And it may still be said that truth is the consistency of our ideas with themselves. Those ideas are false that are not consistent with the series of ideas that are raised in our minds by, [i. e.,] according to, the order of nature.

Corollary 1. Hence we see in how strict a sense it may be said that God is truth itself.

Corollary 2. Hence it appears that truth consists in having perfect and adequate ideas of things. For instance, if I judge truly how far distant the moon is from the earth, we need not say that this truth consists in the perception of the relation between the two ideas of the moon and the earth, but in the adequateness.

Corollary 3. Hence, certainty is the clear perception of this perfection. Therefore, if we had perfect ideas of all things at once, that is, could have all in one view, we should know all truth at the same moment, and there would be no such thing as ratiocination, or finding out truth. And reasoning is only of use to us in the consequence of the paucity of our ideas and because we can have but very few in view at once. Hence it is evident that all things are self-evident to God.

* * *

Prejudice. Those ideas which do not pertain to the prime essence of things — such as all colors that are everywhere objected to our eyes; and sounds that are continually in our ears; those that affect the touch, as cold and heats; and all our sensations — exceedingly clog the mind in searching into the innermost nature of things, and cast such a mist over things that there is need of a sharp sight to see clearly through. For these will be con-

tinually in the mind and associated with other ideas, let us be thinking of what we will. And it is a continual care and pains to keep clear of their entanglements in our scrutinies into things. This is one way whereby the body and the senses obscure the views of the mind. The world seems so differently to our eyes, to our ears and other senses, from the idea we have of it by reason that we can hardly realize the latter. . . .

* * *

Personal Identity. Well might Mr. Locke say that identity of person consisted in identity of consciousness, for he might have said that identity of spirit, too, consisted in the same consciousness. For a mind or spirit is nothing else but consciousness and what is included in it. The same consciousness is, to all intents and purposes, individually the very same spirit or substance as much as the same particle of matter can be the same with itself at different times.

John Locke: FREE WILL A MISTAKEN BELIEF

No intellectual debate has raged so long and noisily in western history as the one over the possibilities and limits of human freedom. Before Locke, Hobbes and Leibniz, among many others, had devoted their attention to proving that man wills or chooses not in some arbitrary fashion, but from what is to him the greatest apparent good. Indeed, he cannot choose otherwise. Locke compelled philosophers to take a second look at the historic "faculty" psychology, composed of physical senses, common sense, imagination, memory, reason, will (heart) and passions (viscera). These had been carefully distinguished according to their specific functions, but Locke greatly simplified the lengthy chain reaction which made up mental processes, and broke down the distinctions between them. From this, he progressed further and re-

From John Locke, *An Essay concerning Human Understanding*, vol. I, pp. 325–332, 345–346.

fused to accept the sharp difference usually set between freedom and determinism in the Age of Reason. The following selection is a representative critique of "self-determination" and the one most familiar to Edwards.

WILLING, or volition, being an action, and freedom consisting in a power of acting or not acting, a man in respect of willing [or the act of volition], when any action in his power is once proposed to his thoughts, [as presently to be done,] cannot be free. The reason whereof is very manifest. For, it being unavoidable that the action depending on his will should exist or not exist, and its existence or not existence following perfectly the determination and preference of his will, he cannot avoid willing the existence or non-existence of that action; it is absolutely necessary that he will the one or the other; i. e. prefer the one to the other: since one of them must necessarily follow; and that which does follow follows by the choice and determination of his mind; that is, by his willing it: for if he did not will it, it would not be. So that, in respect of the act of willing, a man [in such a case] is not free: liberty consisting in a power to act or not to act; which, in regard of volition, a man, [upon such a proposal] has not. [For it is unavoidably necessary to prefer the doing or forbearance of an action in a man's power, which is once so proposed to his thoughts; a man must necessarily will the one or the other of them; upon which preference or volition, the action or its forbearance certainly follows, and is truly voluntary. But the act of volition, or preferring one of the two, being that which he cannot avoid, a man, in respect of that act of willing, is under a necessity, and so cannot be free; unless necessity and freedom can consist together, and a man can be free and bound at once.] [Besides to make a man free

after this manner, by making the action of willing to depend on his will, there must be another antecedent will, to determine the acts of this will, and another to determine that, and so *in infinitum:* for wherever one stops, the actions of the last will cannot be free. Nor is any being, as far I can comprehend beings above me, capable of such a freedom of will, that it can forbear to will, i. e. to prefer the being or not being of anything in its power, which it has once considered as such.]

This, then, is evident, That *a man is not at liberty to will, or not to will, anything in his power that he once considers of:* liberty consisting in a power to act or to forbear acting, and in that only. For a man that sits still is said yet to be at liberty; because he can walk if he wills it. A man that walks is at liberty also, not because he walks or moves; but because he can stand still if he wills it. But if a man sitting still has not a power to remove himself, he is not at liberty; so likewise a man falling down a precipice, though in motion, is not at liberty, because he cannot stop that motion if he would. This being so, it is plain that a man that is walking, to whom it is proposed to give off walking, is not at liberty, whether he will determine himself to walk, or give off walking or not: he must necessarily prefer one or the other of them; walking or not walking. And so it is in regard of all other actions in our power [so proposed, which are the far greater number. For, considering the vast number of voluntary actions that succeed one another every moment that we are awake in the course of our lives, there are but few of them that are thought on or proposed to the will, till the time they are to be done; and in all such actions, as I have shown, the mind, in respect of willing,] has not a power to act or not to act, wherein consists liberty. The mind, in that case, has not a power to forbear *willing;* it cannot avoid some determination concerning them, let the consideration be as short, the thought as quick as it will, it either leaves the man in the state he was before thinking, or changes it; continues the action, or puts an end to it. Whereby it is manifest, that *it* orders and directs one, in preference to, or with neglect of the other, and thereby either the continuation or change becomes *unavoidably* voluntary.

Since then it is plain that, in most cases, a man is not at liberty, whether he will or no, (for, when an action in his power is proposed to his thoughts, he *cannot* forbear volition; he *must* determine one way or the other;) the next thing demanded is, — *Whether a man be at liberty to will which of the two he pleases, motion or rest?* This question carries the absurdity of it so manifestly in itself, that one might thereby sufficiently be convinced that liberty concerns not the will. For, to ask whether a man be at liberty to will either motion or rest, speaking or silence, which he pleases, is to ask whether a man can will what he wills, or be pleased with what he is pleased with? A question which, I think, needs no answer: and they who can make a question of it must suppose one will to determine the acts of another, and another to determine that, and so on *in infinitum.*

To avoid these and the like absurdities, nothing can be of greater use than to establish in our minds determined ideas of the things under consideration. If the ideas of liberty and volition were well fixed in our understandings, and carried along with us in our minds, as they ought, through all the questions that are raised about them, I suppose a great part of the difficulties that perplex men's thoughts, and entangle their understandings, would be much easier resolved; and we should perceive where the confused signification of terms, or where the nature of the thing caused the obscurity.

First, then, it is carefully to be remembered, That freedom consists in the dependence of the existence, or not existence of any *action,* upon our *volition* of it; and not in the dependence of any action, or its contrary, on our *preference.* A man standing on a cliff, is at liberty to leap twenty yards downwards into the sea, not because he has a power to do the contrary action, which is to leap twenty yards upwards, for that he cannot do; but he is therefore free, because he has a power to leap or not to leap. But if a greater force than his, either holds him fast, or tumbles him down, he is no longer free in that case; because the doing or forbearance of that particular action is no longer in his power. He that is a close prisoner in a room twenty feet square, being at the north side of his chamber, is at liberty to walk twenty feet southward, because he can walk or not walk it; but is not, at the same time, at liberty to do the contrary, i. e. to walk twenty feet northward.

In this, then, consists *freedom,* viz. in our being able to act or not to act, according as we shall choose or will.

Secondly, we must remember, that *volition* or *willing* is an act of the mind directing its thought to the production of any action, and thereby exerting its power to produce it. To avoid multiplying of words, I would crave leave here, under the word *action,* to comprehend the forbearance too of any action proposed: sitting still, or holding one's peace, when walking or speaking are proposed, though mere forbearances, requiring as much the determination of the will, and being as often weighty in their consequences, as the contrary actions, may, on that consideration, well enough pass for actions too: but this I say, that I may not be mistaken, if (for brevity's sake) I speak thus.

Thirdly, the will being nothing but a power in the mind to direct the operative faculties of a man to motion or rest, as far as they depend on such direction; to the question, What is it determines the will? the true and proper answer is, The mind. For that which determines the general power of directing, to this or that particular direction, is nothing but the agent itself exercising the power it has that particular way. If this answer satisfies not, it is plain the meaning of the question, What determines the will? is this, — What moves the mind, in every particular instance, to determine its general power of directing, to this or that particular motion or rest? And to this I answer, — The motive for continuing in the same state or action, is only the present satisfaction in it; the motive to change is always some uneasiness: nothing setting us upon the change of state, or upon any new action, but some uneasiness. This is the great motive that works on the mind to put it upon action, which for shortness' sake we will call determining of the will, which I shall more at large explain.

But, in the way to it, it will be necessary to premise, that, though I have above endeavoured to express the act of volition, by *choosing, preferring,* and the like terms, that signify desire as well as volition, for want of other words to mark that act of the mind whose proper name

is *willing* or *volition;* yet, it being a very simple act, whosoever desires to understand what it is, will better find it by reflecting on his own mind, and observing what it does when it wills, than by any variety of articulate sounds whatsoever. This caution of being careful not to be misled by expressions that do not enough keep up the difference between the *will* and several acts of the mind that are quite distinct from it, I think the more necessary, because I find the will often confounded with several of the affections, especially *desire,* and one put for the other; and that by men who would not willingly be thought not to have had very distinct notions of things, and not to have writ very clearly about them. This, I imagine, has been no small occasion of obscurity and mistake in this matter; and therefore is, as much as may be, to be avoided. For he that shall turn his thoughts inwards upon what passes in his mind when he wills, shall see that the will or power of volition is conversant about nothing but our own *actions;* terminates there; and reaches no further; and that volition is nothing but that particular determination of the mind, whereby, barely by a thought, the mind endeavours to give rise, continuation, or stop, to any action which it takes to be in its power. This, well considered, plainly shows that the will is perfectly distinguished from desire; which, in the very same action, may have a quite contrary tendency from that which our will sets us upon. A man, whom I cannot deny, may oblige me to use persuasions to another, which, at the same time I am speaking, I may wish may not prevail on him. In this case, it is plain the will and desire run counter. I will the action; that tends one way, whilst my desire tends another, and that the direct contrary way. A man who, by a violent fit of the gout in his limbs, finds a doziness in his head, or a want of appetite in his stomach removed, desires to be eased too of the pain of his feet or hands, (for wherever there is pain, there is a desire to be rid of it,) though yet, whilst he apprehends that the removal of the pain may translate the noxious humour to a more vital part, his will is never determined to any one action that may serve to remove this pain. Whence it is evident that desiring and willing are two distinct acts of the mind; and consequently, that the will, which is but the power of volition, is much more distinct from desire.

* * *

This is so far from being a restraint or diminution of freedom, that it is the very improvement and benefit of it; it is not an abridgment, it is the end and use of our liberty; and the further we are removed from such a determination, the nearer we are to misery and slavery. A perfect indifference in the mind, not determinable by its last judgment of the good or evil that is thought to attend its choice, would be so far from being an advantage and excellency of any intellectual nature, that it would be as great an imperfection, as the want of indifferency to act, or not to act, till determined by the will, would be an imperfection on the other side. A man is at liberty to lift up his hand to his head, or let it rest quiet: he is perfectly indifferent in either;

and it would be an imperfection in him, if he wanted that power, if he were deprived of that indifferency. But it would be as great an imperfection, if he had the same indifferency, whether he would prefer the lifting up his hand, or its remaining in rest, when it would save his head or eyes from a blow he sees coming: it is as much a perfection, that desire, or the power of preferring, should be determined by good, as that the power of acting should be determined by the will; and the certainer such determination is, the greater is the perfection. Nay, were we determined by anything but the last result of our own minds, judging of the good or evil of any action, we were not free; [the very end of our freedom being, that we may attain the good we choose. And therefore, every man is put under a necessity, by his constitution as an intelligent being, to be determined in willing by his own thought and judgment what is best for him to do: else he would be under the determination of some other than himself, which is want of liberty. And to deny that a man's will, in every determination, follows his own judgment, is to say, that a man wills and acts for an end that he would not have, at the time that he wills and acts for it. For if he prefers it in his present thoughts before any other, it is plain he then thinks better of it, and would have it before any other; unless he can have and not have it, will and not will it, at the same time; a contradiction too manifest to be admitted.]

Jonathan Edwards: FREE WILL IS NOT LOGICAL, MORAL OR TRUE

Deeply disturbed by what he believed to be a popular but false preaching of "free will" against God's providence by the liberal Arminians, Edwards in 1754 published his most famous work. It is probably the most rigorous and devastating attack ever mounted against "liberty of indifference without necessity." Locke had maintained that self-determination was "unphilosophical, self-contradictory, and absurd," and Edwards agreed. As he set out to demolish any notion of man's ability freely to participate in his own salvation, Edwards' defense of original sin and divine election rings of Augustine or Calvin. Theologically, if men have liberty of will, all human actions take place by sheer chance and God is not sovereign, but merely a fence-mender in a disorderly universe. Philosophically, logic and morality require that the will be not a free and disconnected faculty, but always it must act upon the greatest known good in a tight cause-and-effect relationship. To do as one pleases is just the point. In a self-determining will, one's pleasure, or motive, makes no difference. Ironically, Edwards defended traditional doctrines on the basis of the new psychology, while his "liberal" critics still used the older, pre-Lockean faculty psychology. Also, Edwards goes beyond Locke by abolishing strictly differentiated faculties. There is no difference between "preference" in the understanding, and "action" in the will, a point which he develops further in the Religious Affections *(1764).*

WITH RESPECT to that grand inquiry, What determines the Will? it would be very tedious and unnecessary at present to enumerate and examine all the various opinions which have been advanced concerning this matter; nor is it needful that I should enter into a particular disquisition of all points debated in disputes on that question, whether the Will always follows the last dictate of the understanding. It is sufficient to my present purpose to say, it is that motive, which, as it stands in the view of the mind, is the strongest, that determines the Will. But it may be necessary that I should a little explain my meaning in this.

By *motive*, I mean the whole of that which moves, excites or invites the mind to volition, whether that be one thing singly, or many things conjunctly. Many particular things may concur and unite their strength to induce the mind; and, when it is so, all together are as it were one complex motive. And when I speak of the *strongest motive*, I have respect to the strength of the whole that operates to induce to a particular act of volition, whether that be the strength of one thing alone, or of many together.

Whatever is a motive, in this sense, must be something that is extant in the view or apprehension of the understanding, or perceiving faculty. Nothing can

From Jonathan Edwards, *A Careful and Strict Inquiry into the Prevailing Notions of the Freedom of the Will*, in *The Works of President Edwards* (New York: Leavitt and Allen, 1857, 4 vols.), vol. II, pp. 3–4, 7–8, 14–19.

induce or invite the mind to will or act any thing, any further than it is perceived, or is some way or other in the mind's view; for what is wholly unperceived, and perfectly out of the mind's view, cannot affect the mind at all. It is most evident, that nothing is in the mind, or reaches it, or takes any hold of it, any otherwise than as it is perceived or thought of.

And I think it must also be allowed by all, that every thing that is properly called a motive, excitement or inducement to a perceiving, willing agent, has some sort and degree of *tendency* or *advantage* to move or excite the Will, previous to the effect, or to the act of the Will excited. This previous tendency of the motive is what I call the strength of the motive. That motive which has a less degree of previous advantage or tendency to move the Will, or that appears less inviting, as it stands in the view of the mind, is what I call a *weaker motive*. On the contrary, that which appears most inviting, and has, by what appears concerning it to the understanding or apprehension, the greatest degree of previous tendency to excite and induce the choice, is what I call the *strongest motive*. And in this sense, I suppose the Will is always determined by the strongest motive.

Things that exist in the view of the mind have their strength, tendency or advantage to move or excite its Will, from many things appertaining to the nature and circumstances of the thing viewed, the nature and circumstances of the mind that views, and the degree and manner of its view; of which it would perhaps be hard to make a perfect enumeration. But so much I think may be determined in general, without room for controversy, that whatever is perceived or apprehended by an intelligent and voluntary agent, which has the nature and influence of a motive to volition or choice, is considered or viewed as good; nor has it any tendency to invite or engage the election of the soul in any further degree than it appears such. For to say otherwise, would be to say, that things that appear have a tendency by the appearance they make, to engage the mind to elect them, some other way than by their appearing eligible to it; which is absurd. And therefore it must be true, in some sense, that the Will always is as the greatest apparent good is. For the right understanding of this, two things must be well and distinctly observed.

1. It must be observed in what sense I use the term *good;* namely, as of the same import with *agreeable*. To appear good to the mind, as I use the phrase, is the same as to *appear agreeable,* or *seem pleasing* to the mind. Certainly nothing appears inviting and eligible to the mind, or tending to engage its inclination and choice, considered as evil or disagreeable; nor, indeed, as indifferent, and neither agreeable nor disagreeable. But if it tends to draw the inclination, and move the Will, it must be under the notion of that which suits the mind. And therefore that must have the greatest tendency to attract and engage it, which, as it stands in the mind's view, suits it best, and pleases it most; and in that sense, is the greatest apparent good: to say otherwise, is little, if any thing, short of a direct and plain contradiction.

The word *good*, in this sense, includes in its signification, the removal or avoiding of evil, or of that which is disagreeable and uneasy. It is agreeable and pleasing to avoid what is disagreeable and displeasing, and to have uneasiness removed. So that here is included what Mr. Locke supposes determines the Will. For when he speaks of uneasiness as determining the Will, he must be understood as supposing that the end or aim which governs in the volition or act of preference, is the avoiding or removal of that uneasiness; and that is the same thing as choosing and seeking what is more easy and agreeable.

2. When I say, the Will is as the greatest apparent good is, or (as I have explained it) that volition has always for its object the thing which appears most agreeable; it must be carefully observed, to avoid confusion and needless objection, that I speak of the *direct* and *immediate* object of the act of volition; and not some object that the act of Will has not an immediate, but only an indirect and remote respect to. Many acts of volition have some remote relation to an object, that is different from the thing most immediately willed and chosen. Thus, when a drunkard has his liquor before him, and he has to choose whether to drink it or no; the proper and immediate objects, about which his present volition is conversant, and between which his choice now decides, are his own acts, in drinking the liquor, or letting it alone; and this will certainly be done according to what, in the present view of his mind, taken in the whole of it, is most agreeable to him. If he chooses or wills to drink it, and not to let it alone; then this action, as it stands in the view of his mind, with all that belongs to its appearance there, is more agreeable and pleasing than letting it alone.

But the objects to which this act of volition may relate more remotely, and between which his choice may determine more indirectly, are the present pleasure the man expects by drinking, and the future misery which he judges will be the consequence of it: he may judge that this future misery when it comes, will be more disagreeable and unpleasant,

than refraining from drinking now would be. But these two things are not the proper objects that the act of volition spoken of is nextly conversant about. For the act of Will spoken of is concerning present drinking or forbearing to drink. If he wills to drink, then drinking is the proper object of the act of his Will; and drinking, on some account or other, now appears most agreeable to him, and suits him best. If he chooses to refrain, then refraining is the immediate object of his Will, and is most pleasing to him. If in the choice he makes in the case, he prefers a present pleasure to a future advantage, which he judges will be greater when it comes; then a lesser present pleasure appears more agreeable to him than a greater advantage at a distance. If, on the contrary, a future advantage is preferred, then that appears most agreeable, and suits him best. And so still the present volition is as the greatest apparent good at present is.

* * *

Volition, in no one instance that can be mentioned, is otherwise than the greatest apparent good is, in the manner which has been explained. The choice of the mind never departs from that which at that time, and with respect to the direct and immediate objects of that decision of the mind, appears most agreeable and pleasing, all things considered. If the immediate objects of the Will are a man's own actions, then those actions which appear most agreeable to him he wills. If it be now most agreeable to him, all things considered, to walk, then he wills to walk. If it be now, upon the whole of what at present appears to him, most agreeable to speak, then he chooses to speak: if it suits him best to keep silence, then he chooses to keep silence.

There is scarcely a plainer and more universal dictate of the sense and experience of mankind, than that, when men act voluntarily, and do what they please, then they do what suits them best, or what is most agreeable to them. To say, that they do what they please, or what pleases them, but yet do not do what is agreeable to them, is the same thing as to say they do what they please, but do not act their pleasure; and that is to say, that they do what they please, and yet do not do what they please.

It appears from these things, that in some sense, the Will always follows the last dictate of the understanding. But then the understanding must be taken in a large sense, as including the whole faculty of perception or apprehension, and not merely what is called reason or judgment. If by the dictate of the understanding is meant what reason declares to be best or most for the person's happiness, taking in the whole of his duration, it is not true, that the Will always follows the last dictate of the understanding. Such a dictate of reason is quite a different matter from things appearing now most agreeable; all things being put together which pertain to the mind's present perceptions, apprehensions or ideas, in any respect. Although that dictate of reason, when it takes place, is one thing that is put into the scales, and is to be considered as a thing that has concern in the compound influence which moves and induces the Will; and is one thing that is to be considered in estimating the degree of that appearance of good which the Will always follows; either as having its influence added to other things, or subducted from them. When it concurs with other things, then its weight is added to them, as put into the same scale; but when it is against them, it is as a weight in the opposite scale, where

it resists the influence of other things: yet its resistance is often overcome by their greater weight, and so the act of the Will is determined in opposition to it.

* * *

The plain and obvious meaning of the words *Freedom* and *Liberty*, in common speech, is *power, opportunity or advantage, that any one has, to do as he pleases.* Or in other words, his being free from hinderance or impediment in the way of doing, or conducting in any respect, as he wills. And the contrary to Liberty, whatever name we call that by, is a person's being hindered or unable to conduct as he will, or being necessitated to do otherwise.

If this which I have mentioned be the meaning of the word Liberty, in the ordinary use of language; as I trust that none that has ever learned to talk, and is unprejudiced, will deny; then it will follow, that in propriety of speech, neither Liberty, nor its contrary, can properly be ascribed to any being or thing, but that which has such a faculty, power or property, as is called will. For that which is possessed of no such thing as will, cannot have any power or opportunity of doing according to its will, nor be necessitated to act contrary to its will, nor be restrained from acting agreeably to it. And therefore to talk of Liberty, or the contrary, as belonging to the very will itself, is not to speak good sense; it we judge of sense, and nonsense, by the original and proper signification of words. For the will itself is not an agent that has a will: the power of choosing itself, has not a power of choosing. That which has the power of volition or choice is the man or the soul, and not the power of volition itself. And he that has the Liberty of doing according to his will, is the agent or doer who is possessed of the will; and not the will which he is possessed of. We say with propriety, that a bird let loose has power and Liberty to fly; but not that the bird's power of flying has a power and Liberty of flying. To be free is the property of an agent, who is possessed of powers and faculties, as much as to be cunning, valiant, bountiful, or zealous. But these qualities are the properties of men or persons and not the properties of properties.

There are two things that are contrary to this which is called Liberty in common speech. One is constraint; the same is called force, compulsion, and coaction; which is a person's being necessitated to do a thing contrary to his will. The other is restraint; which is his being hindered, and not having power to do according to his will. But that which has no will, cannot be the subject of these things. I need say the less on this head, Mr. Locke having set the same thing forth, with so great clearness, in his *Essay on the Human Understanding.*

But one thing more I would observe concerning what is vulgarly called Liberty; namely, that power and opportunity for one to do and conduct as he will, or according to his choice, is all that is meant by it; without taking into the meaning of the word anything of the cause or original of that choice; or at all considering how the person came to have such a volition; whether it was caused by some external motive or internal habitual bias; whether it was determined by some internal antecedent volition, or whether it happened without a cause; whether it was necessarily connected with something foregoing, or not connected. Let the person come by his volition or choice how he will, yet, if he is able, and there is nothing in the way to

hinder his pursuing and executing his will, the man is fully and perfectly free, according to the primary and common notion of freedom.

What has been said may be sufficient to show what is meant by Liberty, according to the common notions of mankind, and in the usual and primary acceptation of the word: but the word, as used by Arminians, Pelagians and others, who oppose the Calvinists, has an entirely different signification. These several things belong to their notion of Liberty. 1. That it consists in a self-determining power in the will, or a certain sovereignty the will has over itself, and its own acts, whereby it determines its own volitions; so as not to be dependent in its determinations, on any cause without itself, nor determined by any thing prior to its own acts. 2. Indifference belongs to Liberty in their notion of it, or that the mind, previous to the act of volition, be in equilibrio. 3. Contingence is another thing that belongs and is essential to it; not in the common acceptation of the word, as that has been already explained, but as opposed to all necessity, or any fixed and certain connection with some previous ground or reason of its existence. They suppose the essence of Liberty so much to consist in these things, that unless the will of man be free in this sense, he has no real freedom, how much soever he may be at Liberty to act according to his will.

If to evade the force of what has been observed, it should be said, that when the *Arminians* speak of the Will's determining its own acts, they do not mean that the Will determines its acts by any preceding act, or that one act of the Will determines another; but only that the faculty or power of Will, or the soul in the use of that power, determines its own volitions; and that it does it without any act going before the act determined; such an evasion would be full of gross absurdity. — I confess, it is an evasion of my own inventing, and I do not know but I should wrong the *Arminians*, in supposing that any of them would make use of it. But it being as good a one as I can invent, I would observe upon it a few things.

FIRST. If the faculty or power of the Will determines an act of volition, or the soul in the use or exercise of that power, determines it, that is the same thing as for the soul to determine volition by an act of the Will. For an exercise of the power of Will, and an act of that power, are the same thing. Therefore to say, that the power of Will, or the soul in the use or exercise of that power, determines volition, without an act of Will preceding the volition determined, is a contradiction.

SECONDLY. If a power of Will determines the act of the Will, then a power of choosing determines it. For, as was before observed, in every act of Will, there is a choice, and a power of willing is a power of choosing. But if a power of choosing determines the act of volition, it determines it by choosing it. For it is most absurd to say, that a power of choosing determines one thing rather than another, without choosing any thing. But if a power of choosing determines volition by choosing it, then here is the act of volition determined by an antecedent choice, choosing that volition.

THIRDLY. To say, the faculty, or the soul, determines its own volitions, but not by any act, is a contradiction. Because, for the soul to direct, decide, or determine any thing, is to act; and this is supposed; for the soul is here spoken of as being a cause in this affair, bringing something to pass, or doing something; or which is the same thing, exerting itself

in order to an effect, which effect is the determination of volition, or the particular kind and manner of an act of Will. But certainly this exertion or action is not the same with the effect, in order to the production of which it is exerted, but must be something prior to it. . . .

If Arminian liberty of Will, consisting in the Will's determining its own acts, be maintained, the old absurdity and contradiction must be maintained, that every free act of the Will is caused and determined by a foregoing free act of Will; which doth not consist with the free acts arising without any cause, and being so contingent, as not to be fixed by any thing foregoing. So that this evasion must be given up, as not at all relieving, and as that which, instead of supporting this sort of liberty, directly destroys it.

And if it should be supposed, that the soul determines its own acts of Will some other way, than by a foregoing act of Will; still it will not help the cause of their liberty of Will. If it determines them by an act of the understanding, or some other power, then the Will does not determine itself; and so the self-determining power of the Will is given up. And what liberty is there exercised according to their own opinion of liberty, by the soul's being determined by something besides its own choice? The acts of the Will, it is true, may be directed, and effectually determined and fixed; but it is not done by the soul's own will and pleasure: there is no exercise at all of choice or Will in producing the effect: and if Will and choice are not exercised in it, how is the liberty of the Will exercised in it?

So that let Arminians turn which way they please with their notion of liberty, consisting in the Will's determining its own acts, their notion destroys itself. If they hold every free act of Will to be determined by the soul's own free choice, or foregoing free act of Will; foregoing, either in the order of time, or nature; it implies that gross contradiction, that the first free act belonging to the affair, is determined by a free act which is before it. Or if they say, that the free acts of the Will are determined by some other act of the soul, and not an act of Will or choice; this also destroys their notion of liberty, consisting in the acts of the Will being determined by the Will itself; or if they hold that the acts of the Will are determined by nothing at all that is prior to them, but that they are contingent in that sense, that they are determined and fixed by no cause at all; this also destroys their notion of liberty, consisting in the Will's determining its own acts.

II. A MODERN HISTORIAN'S REAPPRAISAL AND HIS CRITIC

Perry Miller: JONATHAN EDWARDS: THE FIRST MODERN AMERICAN

The late Perry Miller brought a major turnabout in American history by his reappraisal of New England Puritanism in which he pointed to many positive and important contributions made by Puritanism to the new republic. His 1949 intellectual biography did the same for Jonathan Edwards. It compelled considerable revision of the long-standing impression that Edwards was a narrow-minded, grim and old-fashioned Calvinist. Miller's argument is based upon the fact that Edwards read Newton and Locke as well as the Puritan divines. He was a theologian on the surface, Miller tells us, but at heart a modern empirical and idealist philosopher of the first water. Indeed, Edwards was so advanced that he alone was truly "liberal" in his day, and twentieth-century men are still catching up with some elements of his thought. Miller wrote what is surely the most important book on Jonathan Edwards, at least in terms of the effect it had in convincing other scholars that Edwards was more a product of the new thought of the Enlightenment than Puritan traditionalism.

THE TRUTH IS, Edwards was infinitely more than a theologian. He was one of America's five or six major artists, who happened to work with ideas instead of with poems or novels. He was much more a psychologist and a poet than a logician, and though he devoted his genius to topics derived from the body of divinity — the will, virtue, sin — he treated them in the manner of the very finest speculators, in the manner of Augustine, Aquinas, and Pascal, as problems not of dogma but of life. Furthermore, the conditions under which he labored, in pioneer America, make his achievement the more remarkable, and his failures the more poignant, not as an episode in the history of creeds and systems, but as a prefiguration of the artist in America. He is the child of genius in this civilization; though he met the forces of our society in their infancy, when they had not yet enlarged into the complexity we now endure, he called them by their names, and pronounced as one foreseeing their tendencies. If the student penetrates behind the technical language, he discovers an intelligence which, as much as Emerson's, Melville's, or Mark Twain's, is both an index of American society and a comment upon it.

If I read him correctly — though Edwards remains, as he was even to himself, an enigma — he repays study because, while he speaks from a primitive religious conception which often seems

From Perry Miller, *Jonathan Edwards* (New York: William Sloan Associates, 1949), pp. xii–xiii, 45–46, 52–57, 71–75, 77–80, 147–149, 156–163, 186–188. Reprinted by permission of William Morrow and Company, Inc.

hopelessly out of touch with even his own day, yet at the same time he speaks from an insight into science and psychology so much ahead of his time that our own can hardly be said to have caught up with him. Though he had followers, he was not the sort of artist who really can found a "school." He is unique, an aboriginal and monolithic power, with nothing of that humanity which opens every heart to Franklin; but he is a reminder that, although our civilization has chosen to wander in the more genial meadows to which Franklin beckoned it, there come periods, either through disaster or through self-knowledge, when applied science and Benjamin Franklin's *The Way to Wealth* seem not a sufficient philosophy of national life.

* * *

. . . He always exalted experience over reason. He could remember being so young that he thought two objects, one twice as far off as the other, were the same distance away, one above the other; his senses, he reflected, made the same representation of them then as now, and in themselves the senses do not deceive: "The only difference is in *experience*." In his latest thinking he condemned as nonsensical all views that regard reason as a rule superior to experience, that build upon "what our reason would lead us to suppose without, or before experience, . . . even in those matters that afterwards are tried by experience, and wherein experience shews things in a different light from what our reason suggested without experience." The riddle of Edwards is that this (as his townsmen came to believe) monstrously intransigent man scorned the doctrinaire: "History, observation, and experience, are the

things which must determine the question."

In these respects Edwards must be called, as this study will call him, an empiricist. This is not to say, however, that Edwards held tentative hypotheses subject to constant alteration by further experiment. Critics filled with the spirit of modern positivism rashly declare that because at the age of twelve Edwards wrote a masterpiece of microscopic observation upon a species of flying spider, and as an undergraduate put down a series of "Notes on Science" which exhibit a phenomenal mastery of Newton, he was a potential scientist thwarted by his environment and forced into the uncongenial wastes of theology. The precocious piece on the spider does indeed indicate, as his nineteenth-century biographer put it, "a fondness, minutely and critically to investigate the works of nature"; but Edwards went to nature and experience, not in search of the possible, but of the given, of that which cannot be controverted, of that to which reason has access only through perception and pain, that of which logic is the servant and from which dialectic receives its premises. "And thus it is we actually determine, that experience is so good and sure a medium of proof."

* * *

Not only had Jonathan Edwards' converse, unlike that of even more erudite contemporaries, included Locke's *Essay,* but the reading of it had been the central and decisive event in his intellectual life. He discovered it in 1717 when still at Wethersfield, two years after the essay on spiders, and read it with far more pleasure "than the most greedy miser finds, when gathering up handfuls of silver and gold, from some newly discovered treasure." History cannot scrape together out of all America as early as 1717 more than a handful of men who had read the *Essay*, and none with any such realization that the "new way of thinking by ideas" would determine the intellectual career of the eighteenth century. The boy of fourteen grasped in a flash what was to take the free and catholic students of Professor Wigglesworth thirty or forty years to comprehend, that Locke was the master-spirit of the age, and that the *Essay* made everything then being offered at Harvard or Yale as philosophy, psychology, and rhetoric so obsolete that it could no longer be taken seriously.

What prepared Edwards for the insight? At first view nothing in the history of thought is more incongruous than the instinctive seizure by this backwoods adolescent upon the doctrine that emerged from the sophisticated entourage of the first Earl of Shaftesbury, and yet one can, I believe, make out the logic of it. The boy had walked in his father's pasture, looking upon the sky and clouds until "the appearance of every thing was altered" and "there seemed to be, as it were, a calm, sweet, cast, or appearance of divine glory, in almost every thing"; he used to sit and view the moon, "singing forth, with a low voice, my contemplations of the Creator." His mind became "greatly fixed on divine things; almost perpetually in the contemplation of them," until his inability to express what he felt became a torturing clog and a burden: "The inward ardour of my soul, seemed to be hindered and pent up, and could not freely flame out as it would." Then he read Locke, and the divine strategy was revealed to him. God's way, Locke made clear, is indirection, which is the only way, because speaking the unspeakable

is impossible; God works through the concrete and the specific, and the mind (Edwards would add, the regenerate mind) must know enough "to stop when it is at the utmost extent of its tether." The way to cope with the problem was not to raise questions and multiply disputes, as did M.A. candidates in the public "commonplacings" by which they qualified themselves to be ministers in New England, but "to take a survey of our own understandings, examine our own powers, and see to what things they were adapted." Otherwise, we shall either come to a "perfect scepticism" or else "let loose our thoughts in the vast ocean of Being; as if all that boundless extent were the natural and undoubted possession of our understandings, wherein there was nothing exempt from its decisions, or that escaped its comprehension."

For a young man on the verge of drowning in the vast ocean of Being, the disclosure of "this historical, plain method," which gave at last a full account of the ways whereby our understandings attain their notions and which prescribed tests of the certainty of knowledge, was not only a rescue, it was a directive for living. It saved him from the fire of his own intensity, or from the scepticism which in moments of depression seemed the only alternative, by teaching him that the one legitimate field of both speculation and worship is the content of the human mind. Out of his study of Locke, remote as such a result was from Locke's aim of bringing philosophy "into well-bred company and polite conversation," Edwards was able to solve his problem, and (as he believed) the problem of American culture, by achieving a permanent and abiding sense "how meet and suitable it was that God should govern the world, and order all things according to his own pleasure."

From the beginning Puritan education was organized into a hierarchy of the liberal arts culminating in a blueprint of creation, taught as the crowning subject in the curriculum and called "technologia," which was supposed to be an organon of all the arts and was therefore an exhaustive chart of the order by which God did govern the world. Therein were laid out all things, concepts, relations, propositions, principles, as in a graph which, with endless branches and subdivisions and "dichotomies," looked like a genealogist's diagram of some gigantic family tree. At the moment he read Locke, Edwards was learning technologia from Elisha Williams. Locke showed him that technologia was "some of the rubbish that lies in the way of knowledge," a "learned but frivolous use of uncouth, affected, or unintelligible terms" that had to be cleared away before the "master-builders" — Locke mentioned specifically Boyle, Sydenham, Huygens, "and the incomparable Mr. Newton," names that echoed ominously in the air of Wethersfield — might get on with the proper business of philosophy, "which is nothing but the true knowledge of things."

The elaborate structure of technologia, which was taught not as a knowledge of things but of "arguments," collapsed in Edwards' mind like a house of cards as he learned from Locke that men can acquire the materials of reason and knowledge solely from (Locke printed it in capitals) "EXPERIENCE." Men have to deal with things, but not with things as they lie in the divine mind or float in the ocean of being, but simply as they are registered on the human brain. When perceived by the mind, a thing is, to speak accurately, no longer just a dead thing by itself, but the mind's "idea" of it. An idea, said Locke, is "the *object* of the understanding when a man thinks." This is, in fact, only common sense, but the point is that one does not need an elaborate scholastic ritual to grasp the definition of ideas: "every one is conscious of them in himself." Yet just that simplicity of the first principle was what delivered Edwards from the maze of technologia a generation in advance of his fellows. Thenceforth Edwards' fundamental premise was Locke's, the assurance that what the mind knows is no more than its ideas, and consequently (Locke again resorted to capitals) that "this great source of most of the ideas we have, depending wholly upon our senses, and derived by them to the understanding, I call SENSATION."

Edwards read this work with ecstasy, the burden of an insupportable weight lifted with every page. No longer, he saw, need mankind struggle through life on the supposition that certain innate concepts were implanted in them which did not originate out of the world about them, which were supposed to be part of the image of God and therefore to exert absolute authority in advance of any experience or any actual problem. Locke made it evident that to believe in such an imperative was to submit to something so out of kilter that it was bound to become an excuse for self-indulgence. Hence Edwards' thought cohered firmly about the basic certainty that God does not impart ideas or obligations outside sense experience, He does not rend the fabric of nature or break the connection between experience and behavior. The universe is all of a piece, and in it God works upon man through the daily shock of sensation, which (here Locke resorted to italics) *"is such an impression or motion made in some part of the body, as produces some perception in the understanding."*

The best of it was, for Edwards, that Locke accounted for, even while destroying, such monstrosities as technologia: those sublime constructions, "which tower above the clouds, and reach as high as heaven itself," all take their rise from (and so can be resolved back into) the lowly senses; "in all that great extent wherein the mind wanders, in those remote speculations it may seem to be elevated with, it stirs not one jot beyond those ideas which *sense* or *reflection* have offered for its contemplation." Therefore Edwards was enabled to understand the predicament of New England civilization: if religion remained bound to an antiquated metaphysic, false philosophy would drag theology deeper into the morass. The free and catholic spirit, confessing by its scorn of cramming principles down another man's throat that it had no principles to cram, was setting up an ideal of candor attached to no particular scheme, a position which was as great an evasion of sensation as the rubbish of technologia. Here was the secret of that decline of piety which all the clergy lamented, but which none was able to arrest.

Furthermore, did not Locke, by supplying the diagnosis, also point the way to rectification: "As the bodies that surround us do diversely affect our organs, the mind is forced to receive the impressions; and cannot avoid the perception of those ideas that are annexed to them." If the way to make living impressions on the minds of men is through the senses, did it not follow that a Christian oratory which would put aside all those vague and insignificant forms of speech, all those abuses of language that have passed for science, which with the help of Locke would "break in upon the sanctuary of vanity and ignorance," which would use words as God uses objects, to force sensations and the ideas annexed to them into men's minds through the only channel ideas can be carried to them, through the senses — would such an oratory not force upon New England the awakening that three generations of prophets had called for in vain? It was central to Locke's analysis that the mind, having no innate faculties of its own, is so dependent upon the outer world that it is wholly passive in receiving impressions, "and whether or no it will have these beginnings, and as it were materials of knowledge, is not in its own power."

Critics of Locke, even in his own day and more ardently in the nineteenth century, have called his doctrine of "passivity" the fatal weakness of empirical psychology; the mind of Edwards, however, was trained by the doctrine of New England, in which it had always been held that man is passive in the reception of grace and that he is bound to sin if he tries to earn salvation by his own efforts or on his own terms. Was it not precisely here that the new metaphysics and the old theology, the modern psychology and the ancient regeneration, came together in an exhilarating union? The whole reach of the vision unfolded before Edwards as he read Locke's innocent observation that simple ideas, "when offered to the mind, the understanding can no more refuse to have, nor alter when they are imprinted, nor blot them out and make new ones itself, than a mirror can refuse, alter, or obliterate the images or ideas which the objects set before it do therein produce." The empirical passivity became for Edwards, in the context of eighteenth-century New England, not an invitation to lethargy, but a program of action.

*　*　*

. . . Edwards could hold in his hands the actual *Principia* and *Opticks* Newton himself took down from his shelves and gave to Dummer for a gift to the new college in the wilderness. (In 1723 Harvard owned the *Opticks* but no *Principia.*) We know that Samuel Johnson read this *Principia* and vainly tried to teach himself enough mathematics to understand it. Edwards never understood fluxions or other higher mathematics, but to the extent that a man can read Newton without such proficiency, he read him, and though like most admirers he accepted the "sublime geometry" on Newton's say-so, he appreciated the more literary "Scholia" with a profundity not to be rivaled in America until the great John Winthrop took over the Hollis professorship as successor to Greenwood in 1738, or until a printer in Philadelphia succeeded in keeping his shop until it kept him in sufficient leisure to allow time for reading. Consequently, when we go behind Edwards' early publications to find the hidden meanings, we discover in the "Notes" not one key but two, a dual series of reflections, often intermingled but not yet synthesized. The one proceeds out of Locke and becomes what posterity has called his "idealism"; the other begins with Newton and becomes what has been less widely appreciated, his naturalism. In his mind there was an equilibrium, more or less stable, of the two, which is the background of his cabalistic dichotomy, set up in the Boston lecture as though it were too apparent to need explaining; if his proposition about the "inherent good" requires for full comprehension a knowledge of Locke, his assertion of the "objective good" demands an equally rigorous study of Newton.

Edwards would not compartmentalize his thinking. He is the last great American, perhaps the last European, for whom there could be no warfare between religion and science, or between ethics and nature. He was incapable of accepting Christianity and physics on separate premises. His mind was so constituted — call it courage or call it naïveté — that he went directly to the issues of his age, defined them, and asserted the historic Protestant doctrine in full cognizance of the latest disclosures in both psychology and natural science. That the psychology he accepted was an oversimplified sensationalism, and that his science was unaware of evolution and relativity, should not obscure the fact that in both quarters he dealt with the primary intellectual achievements of modernism, with the assumptions upon which our psychology and physics still prosper: that man is conditioned and that the universe is uniform law. The importance of Edwards — I cannot insist too strongly — lies not in his answers, which often are pathetic testimonies to his lack of sophistication or to the meagerness of his resources, but in his inspired definitions. Locke is, after all, the father of modern psychology, and Newton is the fountainhead of our physics; their American student, aided by remoteness, by technological innocence, and undoubtedly by his arrogance, asked in all cogency why, if the human organism is a protoplasm molded by environment, and if its environment is a system of unalterable operations, need mankind any longer agonize, as they had for seventeen hundred years, over the burden of sin? By defining the meaning of terms derived from Locke and Newton in the light of this question, Edwards established certain readings so profound that only from the perspective of today can they be fully appreciated.

"The whole burden of philosophy,"

said Newton, "seems to consist in this — from the phenomena of motions to investigate the forces of nature, and then from these forces to demonstrate the other phenomena." Conceiving the universe as motion — which, unlike the concepts hitherto taught in New England, such as substance, form, and accident, could be expressed in mathematical formulae — Newton arrived at such an earth-shaking discovery as this: "If you press a stone with your finger, the finger is also pressed by the stone." Of course, no farmer in Connecticut needed to be told, "If a horse draws a stone tied to a rope, the horse (if I may say so) will be equally drawn back towards the stone." But every farmer was told, and professed to believe, what Luther had put succinctly over a century before the *Principia:* "For though you were nothing but good works from the sole of your foot to the crown of your head, yet you would not be righteous, nor worship God, nor fulfill the First Commandment, since God cannot be worshipped unless you ascribe to Him the glory of truthfulness and of all goodness, which is due Him." By the logic of that other science, called divinity or theology, upon which New England was founded, the best of deeds were "insensate things," which in themselves reflect no slightest glory upon the Creator. "Faith alone is the righteousness of a Christian man." If a man has faith, according to Luther — and after him Calvin and the Puritans — he "is free from all things and over all things."

For a century Yankees had believed this, but they had not been free from and over such things as the stones in their pastures, which broke both their own and their horses' backs. In the old-fashioned physics a stone was a concatenation of form and substance, with a final cause, and so its weight could be "im-

proved" in theology as a trial laid upon man in punishment of his sin; but if now the obstinacy of the resisting body was an inherent mathematical product of its density and its bulk, if it lawfully possessed an inertia of its own which man must comprehend by the analogy of muscular effort, how could a man struggling with a rock in his field become persuaded that by faith he might be "free" of it? A more logical conclusion was that since weight is a natural force, the profitable method of freeing himself from it was by the law of levers, by a better breed of horses, but not by moralizing that the presumption of good works means the instant loss of faith and its benefits. There was — as Edwards perceived the situation — an organic connection between Newton's laws of motion and that law of salvation by faith which Calvin had made, once and for all, "the principal hinge by which religion is supported."

Luther, Calvin, and the founders of New England frequently utilized the physics of their day, which was still scholastic, for illustration or confirmation of their doctrines, but they never dreamed of resting the case for Protestantism upon the laws of nature. Edwards saw in a glance that no theology would any longer survive unless it could be integrated with the *Principia.* Newton claimed that in so far as we can learn the first cause from natural philosophy, "so far our Duty towards Him, as well as towards one another, will appear to us by the Light of Nature." This was not a boast, it was a threat. The *Principia* meant that henceforth there was to be no intelligible order apart from the actual. Although Newton discreetly left unanswered certain basic queries, he did show beyond question that the method of inquiry, in theology no less than in science, must be conformed to physical reality: "For Nature is pleased with simplicity, and affects not the pomp of superfluous causes."

In 1734 Edwards preached a series of sermons on justification by faith, the "principal hinge" of Protestantism; he reworked them into a sustained tract which he published in 1738. It was the most elaborate intellectual production he had yet attempted, and it figures in his development — or rather in the public exhibition of the development he had already undergone — as the first effort in American history to coördinate with the doctrine of Puritan revelation the new concept of science, in which such a superfluity of causes as had been the stock-in-trade of Edwards' predecessors became an affectation of pomp. He was resolved to prove that justification must in all simplicity be merged with the order of causality, and that if salvation was to be called an effect, of which faith was in some sense the cause, then the sequence must be formulated anew in language compatible with Newton's.

* * *

He maneuvered a revolt by substituting for seventeenth-century legalisms the brute language of eighteenth-century physics. He cast off habits of mind formed in feudalism, and entered abruptly into modernity, where facts rather than prescriptive rights and charters were henceforth to be the arbiters of human affairs. If the experience of regeneration is real, then "what is real in the union between Christ and his people, is the foundation of what is legal." The language of revolution in this undramatic sentence is difficult to catch across the centuries, but taken in the context of the 1730's it is as decisive,

and as fundamental, as that of the more historic declarations. In 1734 Edwards was applying to theology a critique which assumed that theology should derive from experience and not from logic or from convention. His society, having slipped into a way of calling faith the condition of a covenant, had made the gratuitous assumption that faith was therefore the actual producer of the effect. It was heedlessly supposing that faith is the cause of salvation, and had insensibly come to assume that a man's belief worked his spiritual character exactly as by his physical exertion he shoved a stone out of a meadow. The people had succumbed to a metaphor, and had taken a shallow analogy for a scientific fact. Hence religion, which can thrive only upon realities, was fallen into decay.

Thus without openly proclaiming a revolution, Edwards effectively staged one. The object of his attack was what his society had hitherto assumed to be the relation of cause to effect, on which assumption it was constructed. If a ball that strikes another is called the cause of motion in the other, it then works the effect and determines the consequences; if, however, the first can be said only to transmit force to the second, it is but the first in a series of events determined by a law higher than itself. Puritanism all unwittingly had made the fatal mistake — it has proved equally disastrous for other cultures — of supposing that an event in one realm can cause effects in a totally other realm, that a man's act of belief can oblige the will of God. It had tried to make the transcendent conform to the finite, and pretended that it had succeeded. Edwards drew upon his study of Newton for a contradictory conception: "There is a difference between being justified by a thing, and that thing universally, and necessarily, and inseparably attending or going with justification." He went to physics for a cause that does not bind the effect by producing it; he found in the new science (few besides Newton himself understood that this was the hidden meaning of the *Principia*) the concept of an antecedent to a subsequent, in which the subsequent, when it does come to pass, proves to be whatever it is by itself and in itself, without determination by the precedent.

He never bewildered his auditors by expounding scientific analogies beyond their grasp, but he quietly took into the realm of theology the principles he had learned — or believed were obvious — in his inspired reading of Newton. Obviously his imagination had taken fire from such remarks of Newton's as, "It is not to be conceived that mere mechanical causes could give birth to so many regular motions." Thousands of Newtonians in the eighteenth and nineteenth centuries took this to mean only that "God" created the universe; Edwards took it to mean that cause in the realm of mechanics is merely a sequence of phenomena, with the inner connection of cause and effect still mysterious and terrifying. He interpreted the sequence of belief and regeneration by the same insight. His people, of course, were still ignorant of the "Notes on the Mind." Had they been permitted to take them from his desk, they might have comprehended how, in his view, the old Aristotelian array of causes — final, formal, and material — had been dissolved before the triumph of the now solitary efficient cause. Hence they might have understood that for him the secret of nature was no longer that an efficient cause of itself works such and such an effect, but is to be defined as "that after or upon the existence of which, or the existence

of it after such a manner, the existence of another thing follows." All effects must therefore have their causes, but no effect is a "result" of what has gone before it.

The metaphysics of this idea were profound, but Edwards' statement is so enigmatic that we may rightly doubt whether many good burghers in Northampton had any notion what he was talking about. Still, the import was clear: a once harsh doctrine, which for over a century had been progressively rendered harmless and comfortable, was once more harsh.

* * *

Edwards scientifically, deliberately, committed Puritanism, which had been a fervent rationalism of the covenant, to a pure passion of the senses, and the terror he imparted was the terror of modern man, the terror of insecurity. He overthrew the kind of religious philosophy that had dominated Western Europe since the fall of Rome, the system wherein there was always — whether in terms of the City of God, or of the Mass and absolution, or of final causes and substantial forms, or, at the last, in terms of the Puritan covenant — an ascertainable basis for human safety. Now there was none:

Unconverted men walk over the pit of hell on a rotten covering, and there are innumerable places in this covering so weak that they will not bear their weight, and these places are not seen. The arrows of death fly unseen at noonday; the sharpest sight cannot discern them.

In the moment of triumph, Edwards threw off disguises and exposed the secret long nurtured; the last remnant of scholasticism was discarded, and God was no longer bound by any promise, whether of metaphysics or of law. Edwards brought mankind, as Protestantism must always bring them, without mitigation, protection, or indulgence, face to face with a cosmos fundamentally inhuman: "There are no means within reach that can be any security to them." They are without any refuge, and "all that preserves them every moment is the mere arbitrary will, and uncovenanted, unobliged forbearance of an incensed God." Edwards' preaching was America's sudden leap into modernity.

The modern student must, if he wishes to comprehend, free himself of certain ultra modern prejudices. Even among the devout, torments are generally considered, in Edwards' word, "bugbears." Were Edwards only a shouting evangelist who drummed up hysteria with hellfire and brimstone, he would pertain to social history along with Asbury and Peter Cartwright, but not to literature and not to philosophy. By supplying a vehicle which ignorance and crudity soon adopted, Edwards wrought incalculable harm, though we must remember that the main current of American revivalism flows from Whitefield and the Methodists rather than from him, and that among revivalists he is a peculiar figure. Edwards was primarily concerned with the problem of communication. By the time of Channing, Emerson, and Horace Bushnell, the terms of this problem were so different from those of the early eighteenth century that they could not understand him; today, the terms forced upon us, albeit more complex, are essentially those that confronted him: a behavioristic psychology and a universe of a-moral forces. Far from being street-corner evangelism, Edwards' sermons are immense and concentrated efforts to get across, in the simplest language, the meaning of the religious life, of the life of consciousness, after physics has reduced nature to a series of irreversible equations, after analysis of the mind has reduced intelligence to sensory conditioning. They are, we may say, explorations of the meaning of meaning.

Not that they are systematic expositions. The terms of art are concealed, and they attempt to solve the problem not by metaphysics but by action. Edwards strove to work so upon his listeners that in the act of comprehension they could not help knowing the answer. They are direct, frontal attacks upon epistemological doubt. Locke condemned enthusiasm for holding ideas without regard to objective fact, and pled for their control by reason; yet he had to confess that by his philosophy no ideas in the mind could ever be "exactly the images and resemblances of something inherent in the subject." How, then, can an idea be called true? How can a perception have moral or passionate value if the sequence of causes is implacably fixed without regard to values? In parrying these questions, Locke hit upon a significant analogy: sensations bear no more likeness to things existing without us "than the names that stand for them are the likeness of our ideas, which yet upon hearing they are apt to excite in us." To his surprise, Locke stumbled upon the discovery that the problem of language is one with the problem of knowledge. Thereupon, further embarrassing questions disclosed themselves: how can language be anything but the chance accumulation of conditioned reflexes? How, in a scientific cosmos, can words be used to regenerate or to unite a society? Edwards' sermons must be read as an effort to meet these questions head-on. They are experimental wrestlings with the two gigantic issues of modern philosophy: of the link between the objective and the subjective; and of semantics itself — of how words can be manipulated so that, despite their radical unlikeness to concepts, they will convey trustworthy ideas.

Of course, Edwards never doubted that a hell exists to which sinners go after death, but that consideration was a footnote.

*　*　*

If a sermon was to work an effect, it had to impart the sensible idea in all immediacy; in the new psychology, it must become, not a traveler's report nor an astrologer's prediction, but an actual descent into hell.

By this road Edwards led New England toward the semantic problem that, in one form or another, challenged everyone around the beginning of the century, and still challenges us. Locke himself only belatedly became aware that it existed, and midway through the *Essay* had to turn aside from his argument to spend Book III on "Words." At first the answer seemed to him simple enough: language in the sensational psychology is wholly artificial; in themselves words are merely noises, and either "pain" or "bread" may signify the staff of life, depending on the convention established in the society. There is absolutely no "natural connexion" between a particular sound and a specific thing; a word has meaning, conveys an idea, only "by a perfect voluntary imposition." Imposition is an act of will, of the corporate will, which is often capricious and subject to fashion. A word is merely "annexed" to reality.

But precisely here difficulties began to accumulate. In the hypothetical state of nature, words might stand for the signs of basic realities, but as society grew more complex, the words would become separated from their objects and lead a life of their own. This was psychologically explicable: the tongue can say the word when no idea is in the mind; the mind itself can take the idea for granted and retain the word after the perception is utterly forgotten. Instead of being annexed to an object, the word itself becomes an object, a pallid object as compared with the thing it stands for, but the only object the mind any longer knows. Children and whole societies — New England for one — can learn the words before they have the experience, and their knowing the words will preclude the experience; thus they drag on for generations, like virgins reading of love in romances, without ever knowing the meanings. The leadership of New England would never arouse virgin souls from formality until it jolted them into a new awareness — a fresh perception — of the primordial oneness of word and idea. Otherwise the orators would induce an ecstasy which is, at best, verbal, which leaves the emotions untouched and gives the listener no more than a pattern of words — sarcasms, insults, derisions — in which the fitting of phrase to phrase proves to be only meticulousness, from which all ulterior reference has vanished. They would scratch men's ears, but never scare their hearts.

By his dissertation on language, Locke had no intention of assisting theologians; instead, he hoped to silence them once and for all. If he could prove that the controversies "which have so laid waste the intellectual world" were nothing but ill-use of words, mere haggling about "mixed modes" (which are not imprints of real things but constructions "put together in the mind, independent from any original patterns in nature"), he could call a halt to "wrangling, without improvement or information." Edwards saw that Locke's satire on the language of theologians — "the voluntary and unsteady signs of their own ideas" — applied to his colleagues, but his admiration for Locke was thereby increased, and Locke was still "a certain great man" despite his hostility to Calvinism because he showed Edwards, if no one else, that New England's problem was primarily linguistic. Edwards read more deeply into Locke than did Locke himself; he put the substance of his penetration into an early resolution: "To extricate all questions from least confusion or ambiguity of words, so that the ideas shall be left naked." Again, the resolution was concealed in the performance, but occasionally he showed his hand: "Sounds and letters are external things," he let slip, "that are the objects of the external senses of seeing and hearing." Hence Edwards' pulpit oratory was a consuming effort to make sounds become objects, to control and discipline his utterance so that words would immediately be registered on the senses not as noises but as ideas. To use the term in its technical rather than its debased sense, his was truly "sensational" preaching, which wrought an overwhelming effect by extraordinary simplicity.

The problem given him by New England society was to make words once more represent a reality other than themselves, but he formulated it out of Locke: if language is inherently conventional, and if in a particular culture it has become wholly conventionalized, how can one employ a convention to shatter conventionality? It could be done only by freeing language from stale associations, by forcing words so to function in the chain of natural causes that out of the shock upon the senses would come ap-

prehension of the idea. Only then could the meaning of meanings be carried to the heart of listeners. Committed by Locke to an environmentalism in which not the nature of the shock but the nature of the recipient determined the kind of effect, Edwards further committed himself to administering the kind of shock that would transform the recipient, by psychological processes, into the kind of person who would absorb the shock in only one way. He was emboldened to this improvement upon his master by Locke's hint that subjective perception is true in so far as it is also perception of reality. The source of human error is not the senses, which never deceive, but an inability or a wanton refusal to comprehend the evidence of the senses. Preaching should address the real culprit: "I am not afraid to tell sinners, that are most sensible of their misery, that their case is indeed miserable as they think it to be, and a thousand times more so; for this is the truth.". . .

Gradually taking shape in this analysis was a radically new definition of the religious man, not as right-thinking, but as "influenced by some affection, either love or hatred, desire, hope, fear." Multitudes may hear the word, none will be altered except those that are affected; good commentaries and rhetorically perfect essays will give men speculative understanding, but make no real impression: "God hath appointed a particular and lively application of his word to men in the preaching of it, as a fit means to affect sinners with the importance of the things of religion, and their own misery, and necessity of a remedy, and the glory and sufficiency of a remedy provided." The parting between heaven and hell is located not in the regions of the sky or under the earth, not even in the Last

Judgment, but in the human perception; the function of art is to make the distinction unmistakable. This requires of the artist a stupendous assertion of will: he must *make* words convey the idea of heaven, he must *force* them to give the idea of hell.

The great moments in Edwards' apocalyptic sermons are such efforts of will. Let us consider another passage, as successful as any in the Enfield sermon, this time without the image of the spider:

We can conceive but little of the matter: we cannot conceive what that sinking of the soul in such a case is. But to help your conception, imagine yourself to be cast into a fiery oven, all of a glowing heat, or into the midst of a glowing brick-kiln, or of a great furnace, where your pain would be as much greater than that occasioned by accidentally touching a coal of fire, as the heat is greater. Imagine also that your body were to lie there for a quarter of an hour, full of fire, as full within and without as a bright coal of fire, all the while full of quick sense; what horror would you feel at the entrance of such a furnace! And how long would that quarter of an hour seem to you! If it were to be measured by a glass, how long would the glass seem to be running! And after you had endured it for one minute, how overbearing would it be to you to think that you had it to endure the other fourteen!

But what would be the effect on your soul, if you knew you must lie there enduring that torment to the full for twenty-four hours! And how much greater would be the effect, if you knew you must endure it for a whole year; and how vastly greater still, if you knew you must endure it for a thousand years! O then, how would your heart sink, if you thought, if you knew, that you must bear it forever and ever! That there would be no end! That after millions of millions of ages, your torment would be no nearer to an end, than ever it was; and that you never, never should be delivered!

The achievement of this passage is the nakedness of the idea. There is no figure of speech (the blunt command to imagine yourself in a brick-kiln is literally the thing, not a simile or a metaphor), nothing pejorative; it is as bare as experience itself, as it would be to the sense that suffers. It is, I take it, what Hermann Broch calls the style of old age, a phrase applicable to Edwards' earliest as to his latest writing, a style reduced to a few prime concepts, that relies on the syntax: the artist who has reached this point, says Broch, is beyond art, "his attitude approximates that of the scientist with whom he shares the concern for expressing the universe." When critics objected that the shrieks and exclamations of his auditors were not signs of the presence of the spirit, Edwards replied from the lofty height of his linguistic science: "Cryings out, . . . as I have seen them from time to time, is as much an evidence to me, of the general cause it proceeds from, as language: I have learned the meaning of it, the same way that persons learn the meaning of language, viz., by use and experience.". . .

In the summer of 1741 Edwards was at the height of his career and influence. Every house in town was full of outcries, faintings, and convulsions; but if there was distress, there was also admiration and joy. He could recite the transformations: young people forsaking frolicking, impure language, and lewd songs; reform in dress and avoidance of taverns; beaux and fine ladies become serious and mortified; throughout New England the Bible in esteem, the Lord's day observed, differences reconciled and faults confessed; old grudges and long-continued breaches made up in entire amity. In Northampton, party spirit so far ceased that town meetings were no longer disfigured by unchristian heats, and, almost too amazing to relate, they came to an agreement about the common lands! If more evidence were needed, the divine power had supported many hearts under great trials, the death of children and extreme pain of body; and finally, proof beyond all proof, under its influence some "have, in such a calm, bright and joyful frame of mind, been carried through the valley of the shadow of death." This indubitably was the work of a general, not of a particular cause, not of mechanics but of reality. "That which is lovely in itself, is lovely when it appears." Such effects could not be wrought by words, but only by ideas; these were not mass hysterias or mob frenzies, but universal subjective conformations, among an entire people, to the objective fact. They were inviolable sequences arising out of a sense of newness and freshness. They were not enthusiasm. If any still doubted — all that winter and spring there was no sign of life from Charles Chauncy — let them face the facts. This was the day of God's visitation. "Experience shows it."

* * *

Western culture has never been uncomfortable when living with the out-and-out supernatural: the mystery of the Mass is frankly mysterious; if grace is an influx of spirit, the people pray for grace as parched counties pray for rain. On the other hand, when conversion is defined as a rational persuasion, those who have the education and the wit manage it, and the others bow to a superiority they cannot understand. But Edwards wove the supernatural into the natural, the rational into the emotional, and thus made the mystery so nearly comprehen-

sible that it became terrifying. He called it a form of perception, and from his description everybody would seem to be capable of it — except that not everybody is. His supernaturalism was naturalized, or if you will, he supernaturalized nature, and introduced the divine element into the world, not as a substance or a quantity, not as a compound of already existing things or an addition to them, but as "what some metaphysicians call a new simple idea."

He wanted desperately to conceal the terms of art, and not bewilder simple people by parading great names like Newton and Locke; but more desperately he needed a vocabulary, and so published grace as a simple idea, an irreducible pellet of experience which has no tangible being and yet is the principle of the organization of being, as light is an organization of color and sweetness an organization of honeys. This new principle, "in a mind, that is a perceiving, thinking conscious thing," being a sensation, is at once a perception, and so "a principle of a new kind of perception or spiritual sensation," without which "all other principles of perception, and all our faculties are useless and vain." This evanescent, universally accessible, and yet seldom seized-upon power — in Edwards' packed statement, it is practically one with consciousness aware of the conscious — he substituted for that which Christianity had hitherto treated as an eternal decree within the economy of the Godhead.

No matter how much he called the new simple idea supernatural, the suspicion then and now is that he meant only that it was not unnatural. He fascinated a few, but outraged more, when he insisted that the idea is no addition to knowledge, no increase in the number of atoms in the universe, no injection of a divine fluid into human veins, not even (except metaphorically) a light. It "is not a new faculty of understanding," it is a new principle of coherence in the soul which immediately becomes the foundation "for a new kind of exercises of the same faculty of understanding." Even "principle" is a dangerous word, which he used "for want of a word of a more determinate signification." It usually connotes something added to the previous store, a new substance materialized out of nowhere, but Edwards' point was that for the truly perceptive there has been no more, possibly even less, of a fund of experience than for others, only

that into such natures, "either old or new," is laid a method of making coherent what before was incoherent. Though it is always available to the natural man, he can no more employ it than "a man without the sense of hearing can conceive of the melody of a tune." It is, said Edwards in a sentence that proved as enigmatic to his followers as to his enemies, "a natural habit or foundation for action." It is inward, supernatural, mysterious — and also scientifically explicable, empirically verifiable: it gives "a personal ability and disposition to exert the faculties in exercise of such a certain kind," it is activity itself, "a new kind of exercises of the same faculty of the will."

Vincent Tomas: EDWARDS' MASTER WAS THE BIBLE, NOT LOCKE

Almost all who read Perry Miller's book applauded the way he rescued Edwards from the prevailing picture of a sour preacher who angrily delayed the liberalizing of the American mind. Vincent Tomas, while equally certain that Edwards had been mistreated by history, joined several other critics in suggesting that Miller had overstated his case, since Miller seemed to say, in paraphrase of Bancroft, "He that would know the workings of the Modern American Mind, and especially the throbbings of its heart, must give his days and nights to the study of Jonathan Edwards." Tomas argues that Edwards, despite his hidden thoughts, was still a creature of the eighteenth century and by no means the first twentieth-century man. Edwards remained entirely a New England divine. He was not an existentialist philosopher or Freudian psychoanalyst. He preoccupied himself with matters of traditional theology and the new revivalism. He defended orthodox Christianity against liberal and rational Arminianism. Tomas does not entirely denounce Miller's thesis, but believes that Edwards' reading of Newton and Locke can only be interpreted in the broader framework of Puritan piety. New England was a place where men still devoted their years to the Bible, church fathers and Puritan divines. Edwards was one of these men.

From Vincent Tomas, "The Modernity of Jonathan Edwards," *New England Quarterly,* XXV (March, 1952), pp. 70–73, 82–83. Reprinted by permission of the *New England Quarterly.*

A PHILOSOPHER living in the eighteenth, or even the twentieth, century would be a "medieval" philosopher if his philosophy placed itself at the service of Scripture and was willing to take orders from it. Nor is the question whether a philosopher is medieval or modern the question whether what he takes to be truths discovered independently of revelation, and which he tries to integrate with revelation, are truths discovered by an ancient like Aristotle or a modern like Newton or Darwin. It is a question of what he does with these truths, and, ultimately, of what his attitude would be if he were forced, as we shall see Edwards was forced, to choose between what he accepts as revealed truth and a truth of reason or of science which is incompatible with it.

. . . Jonathan Edwards is a medieval philosopher. It is simply not true that, as Mr. Miller says, "the peculiar and fascinating character of his achievement is entirely lost if he be not seen as the first and most radical, even though the most tragically misunderstood, of American empiricists." Mr. Miller also says, "Though there were other intellectual influences in his life — Calvin, the traditional body of Puritan science, Cudworth, and Hutcheson — yet Locke and Newton were far and away the dominating sources, and from them he acquired almost all his theoretical starting points," a statement, he adds, "which may seem extreme, [but] is worth emphasizing." We cannot say that this extreme statement is simply not true, since there is some truth in it, but it throws the emphasis the wrong way, in the direction of modernity. How can anyone who has perused Edwards' works fail to mention Scripture as one of the dominating intellectual influences in his life? . . .

The omission of any mention of the Bible from a catalogue of influences on Edwards can only be explained as the result of what Ralph Barton Perry has called the fallacy of difference. "The tendency to conceive a sectarian doctrine in terms of its *special,* to the exclusion of its *generic,* characteristics is important enough to deserve a special name — 'the fallacy of difference.'" It is true that one of the *specific* differences between Edwards and previous Puritans is the presence in his thought of elements that are derived from Newton and Locke. But when Edwards is looked at in the large, and the generic and specific characteristics of his thought are seen in their true proportions and weight, he remains, despite the influence of Newton and Locke, a medieval philosopher, just as Descartes in the large, despite the fact that he incorporated into "inherited principles of medieval philosophy" new conceptions of nature borrowed from the science of *his* day, remains a medieval philosopher. Edwards was a Puritan first, and a Newtonian or Lockean secondarily. As Professor Perry says, "The main body of puritan doctrine, then, is medieval Christianity. In America, it was the chief link of continuity with the medieval past, being a traditional rather than an innovating doctrine. . . . Whereas puritanism taught men to rely on faith, revelation, and authority, and especially on the authority of the Bible as an authentic revelation of the will of God, the Enlightenment proclaimed the accessibility of truth, even basic truths of religion, to the faculty of reason." In these words we find the *generic* characteristics of Edwards. If we drop them out of the picture, what we have left is a grin without a cat. It is by virtue of these characteristics that Edwards, like Puritanism in general, "prolonged in America the medieval Christian view of the world and of human destiny."

. . . There are in Edwards numerous places where he arrives at conclusions unacceptable to the modern mind, by arguments not entirely cogent to the modern mind. Yet these conclusions were credible, and these arguments were cogent, to Edwards. The reason is that he accepted Scripture as revealed truth, and the modern mind does not. In this sense, Edwards "took orders" from Scripture, just as an empiricist will not "take orders" from Scripture, but only from experience.

*　*　*

Before concluding, let us notice a place (there are others) where Edwards was willing to "take orders" from Scripture in a much stronger sense than the one previously described. In *Original Sin* he takes up the objection, made by Taylor and others, that it would be unreasonable if God were to treat Adam and his posterity as if they were one, which God must do if the descendants of Adam deserve punishment for Adam's sin. Just before doing so, and using "fact" in the sense we have described, Edwards says something that Locke would have disapproved of. Locke said, "nothing that is contrary to, and inconsistent with, the clear and self-evident dictates of reason, has a right to be urged or assented to as a matter of faith, wherein reason has nothing to do." But Edwards says, "with respect to this mighty outcry made

against the *reasonableness* of any such *constitution*, by which God is supposed to treat Adam and his posterity as *one*, I would make the following observations. It signifies nothing to exclaim against plain *fact*. . . . Hence, however the matter be attended with difficulty, *fact* obliges us to *get over* it either by finding out some solution, or by shutting our mouths, and acknowledging the weakness and scantiness of our understandings; as we must in other innumerable cases, where apparent and undeniable *fact*, in God's works of creation and providence, is attended with events and circumstances, the *manner* and *reason* of which are difficult to our understandings." He then proceeds to work out the argument which Mr. Miller describes as "the most profound moment in his philosophy," and which so many other commentators have also admired. The argument is that since the existence of every created thing depends at every moment on God's sovereign will, and the identity or oneness of created objects existing through time depends on God's will, therefore there is no difficulty in believing that God can reasonably treat Adam and his posterity as if they were one. Granted its ingenuity, this argument is the desperate expedient of a thinker who was willing to take orders from Scripture as he understood it, and who would "get over" a difficulty that is no difficulty to those for whom reason and experience are a sufficient substitute for revelation. It is, in a word, the argument of a medieval, not a modern, philosopher.

III. EDWARDS THE SCIENTIST

Jonathan Edwards: CONCLUSIONS ON RAYS AND COLORS

In the summer of 1715, when he was but eleven years old, Edwards wrote a remarkably thorough, detailed and accurate account of the balloon or flying spider, entitled, "Of Insects." He was intrigued with the natural world at an early age, and when he studied at Yale, Edwards became a fascinated reader of Newton. There he wrote "Of the Rainbow," and the selection included here, "Colours." It is worthwhile noting that Edwards read Newton with close intensity at a time when the scientist's work still received little attention at English or European universities. Edwards' sympathy with Newton is apparently based upon the young student's avowed desire to know more of God's creation. Newton justified his scientific inquiries on the grounds that knowledge of natural science was an exaltation of the majesty, wisdom and power of God. For both men there was something spiritual about the rational order of the universe, and for both the absolute and universal laws of this universe could be known.

COLOURS. We have already supposed that the different refrangibility of rays arises from their different bulk, we have also supposed that they are very elastic bodies; from these suppositions the colours of natural bodies may be accounted for. That is why some particles of matter reflect such a sort or sorts of rays and no other. The different density of particles whence arises a different attraction and together with their different firmness will account for all. Some bodies have so little of firmness and so easily give way that they are able to resist the stroke of no rays but the least and weakest, and most reflexible rays. All the other rays that are bigger and therefore their force not so easily resisted overcome the resistance of the particles that stand in their way. Such bodies therefore appear blue as the atmosphere or skies, smoke, etc. Again, it is known that the most refrangible rays are most easily attracted, that is, are most easily stayed or diverted by attraction, for as has been already shown refraction and reflection from concave surfaces is by attraction; because therefore that the most refrangible rays are most diverted by refraction and easiest reflected inward from the surface, and most diverted by passing by the edges of bodies, it follows that attraction has most influence on the most refrangible rays.

It is also evident that the particles of bodies that are the most dense have the strongest attraction. The particles of any body therefore may be so dense and attract so strongly as to hold fast all the lesser and more refrangible rays so that they shall none of them be reflected but only the greater rays, on whom the attraction of these particles can have less influence; hereby the body will become red.

From Sereno E. Dwight, *The Life of President Edwards*, pp. 756–757.

And as for the intermediate colours, the particles of a body may be so dense as to hold all the most refrangible rays and may yet not be firm enough to resist the stroke of the least refrangible; hereby the body may become yellow or green or of any other intermediate colour.

Or a body may be coloured by the reflection of a mixture of rays. The body particles may be able to reflect three or four sorts of rays and have too strong an attraction to reflect those rays that are less and too weak a resistance to reflect the bigger rays. Or the colour of a body may be compounded or reflected rays of very distant degrees of refrangibility and not reflect any of the intermediate colours by reason of its being compounded of very heterogeneous particles which have a very different degree of density and firmness. Or the particles of a body may be firm enough to reflect all sorts of rays, yet have so little attraction to hold them that the body will be white. Or a body may be compounded of particles having so little resistance as to reflect no rays, of so great density as to hold all, or so full of pores as to drink in all; then the body is black.

Or the particles of bodies may have pores and hollows that may be big enough to let in the least rays, not the rest; so that the pores of particles may have much to do in the causing of colours.

The blue of mountains at a distance is not made by any rays reflected from the mountains but from the air and vapours that are between us and them. The mountain occasions the blueness by intercepting all rays that would come from beyond to disturb the colour by their mixture.

It may therefore seem a difficulty why the atmosphere all round by the horizon does not appear very blue, seeing it is evident that the atmosphere reflects chiefly the blue rays as appears in the higher parts of the atmosphere by the blueness of the sky, and near the earth by the blueness of mountains, and the redness or yellowness of the rising and setting sun. It would therefore seem that the atmosphere should appear most blue where no rays are intercepted by mountains because the atmosphere beyond the mountain reflects blue rays as well as on this side. Therefore it seems that there would be more blue rays come to our eyes where none were intercepted by mountains. And consequently that the most lively blue would be there. And so it would be, if blue rays came to our eyes in the same proportion as they are reflected. But most of those blue rays that are reflected by those parts of the atmosphere that are at a great distance are intercepted by the intermediate air before they come to our eyes (for the air by supposition intercepts them easiest) and only those few yellow rays and less reflexible rays that are reflected by the air come to our eyes whence it comes to pass that the atmosphere near the horizon does not appear blue but of a whitish yellow. And sometimes when it is filled with more dense exhalations that can reflect less reflexible rays still, it appears a little reddish.

Clarence H. Faust: SCIENCE IN THE INTERESTS OF RELIGION

Many scholars have been intrigued by Edwards' early scientific ventures, particularly as he sought to harmonize the new empirical science with idealist philosophy and Puritan theology. However, in this selection Clarence H. Faust insists that Edwards' interest in true scientific inquiry was quite limited. The natural world drew his attention only when it assisted him in questions of the supernatural world, especially in defense of orthodoxy or revivalism. Faust is critical of other interpreters for paying disproportionate attention to the very small body of scientific writings among Edwards' multivolume works. Perhaps the main question is the effect of Faust's negative argument upon the case for Edwards' modernity.

SERENO E. DWIGHT, writing *The Life of President Edwards* in 1830, remarked that "One characteristic of which he has not generally been suspected, but which he possessed in an unusual degree was a fondness, minutely and critically to investigate the works of nature." Succeeding students of Edwards' works have often reiterated that assertion. Alexander V. G. Allen has said that Edwards was "particularly a keen observer of the mysteries of the outward world and eager to discern its laws." Egbert C. Smyth in an article for *The Andover Review* containing a youthful essay of Edwards on the flying spider, then for the first time published, has quoted Dr. A. S. Packard of Brown University concerning Edwards' "remarkable powers of observation." Dr. Packard's praise, however, is not unqualified. "The most notable fact in the early life of the Connecticut writer," according to I. Woodbridge Riley, "was his precocious possession of the powers both of imagination and of observation." Moses Coit Tyler has spoken of Edwards' "precocity" in physical science, and has set down an impressive list of scientific achievements

credited to him. More recently Mr. Carl Van Doren has characterized Edwards as "a remarkable scientific observer," who "before he was twenty . . . had made important first-hand observations in nature."

Both of the last-named scholars hazard a might-have-been. Tyler believes that if Edwards had given himself to physical science he might have "achieved supreme distinction"; Mr. Van Doren declares that "Without much doubt Edwards would have been the equal of Franklin as a scientist had he continued in such studies, and the two might have divided between them that 'New World of Philosophy' of which both had visions, Edwards excelling in pure, Franklin in applied, science." The miscarriage of Edwards' scientific powers is then laid to theology. "Actually, however," Mr. Van Doren continues, "both departed from their early common ground," and Edwards "went the way of theology, giving up not only natural science but also secular philosophy."

There is evidence, however, that this picture of young Edwards as a "precocious" and "remarkable" scientific observer turning away from his first love,

Clarence H. Faust, "Jonathan Edwards as a Scientist," *American Literature*, I (January, 1930), pp. 393–404. Reprinted by permission of Duke University Press.

science, to embrace theology is in need of revision; and that the picture we should see is that of a man whose career was quite homogeneous, unmarked by any deviation from science into theology, but progressing steadily in a straight line from his juvenile productions, like the letter on the materiality of the soul, to his last great work, *The Freedom of the Will.* Mr. Van Doren, indeed, hints at this when, after saying that Edwards "departed" from science and "went the way of theology," he declares that "Edwards' progression from science and philosophy to theology was in no sense a desertion; the three subjects possessed him side by side, theology perhaps first in time as first in eminence among his intellectual passions."

The notion of Edwards' youthful scientific interest and genius rests upon three legs: the record of some observations of flying spiders written when he was about twelve, some "Notes on Mind" and "Notes on Natural Science" jotted down while he was a student at Yale, and his confession in a *Personal Narrative* that in his youth his "mind had been full of objections against the doctrine of God's sovereignty" but that something had happened to make him embrace Calvinism. To make a just estimate of Edwards' interest in science and of his powers as a scientist it is necessary to examine his so-called scientific work as a whole and to see it in the setting of his life.

When this is done, it becomes clear in the first place that Edwards was never very deeply or exclusively interested in natural science. Before he had written the famous letter on flying spiders he had composed an answer to one who asserted the materiality of the soul, and while he had set down eight pages of foolscap "Notes on Natural Science" at Yale, he

had covered forty-four pages with religious reflections entitled "Miscellanies," and had begun the "Notes on Scripture" which he continued through life. It may be worth noting, too, that Edwards' scientific work was never quite spontaneous. In the case of the letter on spiders, for instance, his father had communicated to a scientific friend, probably in England, an account of some interesting natural curiosity. In his reply the friend had "expressed a desire for any other information of a similar nature." Under this inspiration and the command of his father, Edwards wrote a letter on the flying spider. The "Notes on Natural Science" were composed while studying Abraham Pierson's *Physica* at college, when it was only natural that so inveterate a private scribe as Edwards should have made some record of the ideas stimulated by his class work.

Anything conclusive about Edwards as a scientist must be said, however, on the basis of an examination of his scientific notes themselves. The youthful letter on the flying spider does contain the report of some actual observation, but the most characteristic feature of that letter is the conclusion, in which, following his love of abstract and sweeping generalizations, Edwards asserts that since spiders take to the air only on fair days, and since on such days the wind is always toward the sea, "without doubt almost all aerial insects, and also spiders which live upon trees and are made up of them, are at the end of the year swept away into the sea, and buried in the ocean, and leave nothing behind them but their eggs, for a new stock the next year." Dr. A. S. Packard, commenting on this sweeping assertion, reports his own observations to the contrary.

In another record of these observations of the flying spider, found among Edwards' papers and printed for the first time in 1890, it is significant that almost half of the space is taken up with the statement of theological "Corollaries" of his conclusions about the flying spider. The first of these is: "We hence see the exuberant Goodness of the Creator Who hath not only Provided for all the Necessities but also for the Pleasure and Recreation of all sorts of Creatures And Even the insects and those that are most Despicable." A second corollary is based on Edwards' erroneous conclusion that the flights of spiders eventuate in their destruction: "hence also we may behold and admire at the wisdom Of the Creator and be Convinced from Prvd [Providence] there is exercised about such little things, in this wonderful Contrivance of Annually Carrying of and burying the Corrupting nauseousness of our Air, of which flying insects are little Collections in the bottom of the Ocean where it will Do no harm and Especially the strange way of bringing this About in Spiders (which are Collections of these Collections their food being flying insects) which want wings where it might be done."

In the "Notes on Mind," written at college after a delighted perusal of Locke, we run upon such evidence of Edwards' scientific temper as this paragraph:

32. Angels. Separate Spirits. How far the Angels and Separate Spirits, being in some respects *in place,* in the Third Heaven, where the body of Christ is; their removing from place to place; their coming down from Heaven, then ascending to Heaven; their being with Christ at the Day of Judgment; their seeing bodies; their beholding the Creation of the Material Universe; their having, in their ministry, to do with the bodies of men, with the body of Christ, and other material things; and their seeing God's works of Providence, relating to the Material Universe; — how far these things necessarily imply, that they have some kind of Sensations like ours; and, Whether these things do not show that, by some laws or other, they are united to, some kind of Matter?

Not all of the series of notes on mind is as ludicrously medieval as this, but the passage does illustrate the peril of forming an estimate of Edwards' scientific powers on the basis of the carefully gleaned selections usually published. These notes throughout have a definite theological tinge; and by far the most interesting and significant thing about them is the fact that in this, the earliest section of his notebooks, Edwards is revealed as already addressing himself to the problems which were later to have the sharpest attention of his acutely logical mind — the philosophical aspects of Calvinism, like freedom of the will and original sin. In these notes one sees him already reaching the conclusions which he will later announce and defend so uncompromisingly. Observe these two memoranda.

44. How far the Love of Happiness is the same with the Faculty of the Will. It is not distinct from the mere Capacity of enjoying and suffering, and the Faculty of the Will is no other.

12. Whether any difference between Will and Inclination. Imperative acts of the Will nothing but the prevailing Inclination, concerning what should be done at that moment. So God ordained that the motions of the body should follow that.

This is clearly and precisely the argument of the *Inquiry into the Freedom of Will,* wherein Edwards insists, as in these early notes, that "the will always is what appears most agreeable," and that God foreknows and foreordains thus the volitions of moral agents. In these "Notes on Mind" he also anticipates the greatest difficulty in the philosophy of predestination — moral responsibility. In notes 17 and 18 he raises the question "concerning the prime and proper foundation of Blame," and asks, "How far men may be to blame for their Judgments." A long section of the work on the freedom of the will is devoted to the discussion of the question which these notes raise.

Besides thus anticipating his *magnum opus,* these college notes reveal the fact that Edwards was then already interested in the problem which he later attacked in *The Great Christian Doctrine of Original Sin Defended.* Two paragraphs (numbers 33 and 22) read: "Concerning the greatly weakened Fallibility of the Human Mind in its present state," and "Concerning the corruption of man's nature. How it comes to be corrupt. What is the positive cause for its corruption." These are not questions for investigation, let it be noted, but simply the outline of explanations to be made in the book which he was projecting. Edwards uses few question marks.

In short, then, Edwards began, while in his Junior year at college, aged sixteen, before the date of his supposed "conversion," to plan the great theological works which he was to complete in maturity. Instead of a career sharply divided at the age of eighteen or nineteen, when he is supposed to have "departed" from science and gone "the way of theology," Edwards' path was surprisingly straight. The recognition of this fact carries the implication that his early scientific promise has been much overestimated.

How much Edwards has been overrated as a scientist becomes very evident after an examination of the "Notes on Natural Science." It is upon these eight pages of foolscap that his reputation as a "remarkable scientific observer" mainly rests. It should be explained at the outset that the label "Notes on Natural Science" is not Edwards'. Sereno Dwight, in first publishing, gave them that title, a title which has undoubtedly contributed strength to the impression that as a youth Edwards had a modern scientific spirit, especially since later scholars have sometimes assumed it to be Edwards' own selection.

On the inside cover of the "Notes on Natural Science" Edwards set down some rules to guide him in the writing of a work on natural philosophy. Several of these are rather amusing, as the third in which he decides not to have a preface, but to put whatever is prefatorial "in the body of the work; then I shall be sure to have it read by everyone," and the twelfth in which he resolves in writing to "let there be much compliance with the reader's weakness, and according to the rules in the Ladies Library, Vol. I. p. 340, and Sequel." Several others of the rules which Edwards laid down for himself are valuable in revealing his attitude toward scientific subjects. His plan is to set forth "as many Lemmata, or preparatory propositions, as are necessary, to make the consequent propositions clear and perspicuous," and then to develop "confirming Corollaries and Inferences." He resolves, "in the course of reasoning [the phrase is very significant concerning Edwards' attitude toward science] not to pretend anything to be more certain, than every one will plainly see it is," and "when I would prove anything to take special care that the matter be so stated, that it shall be seen most clearly and distinctly." The whole thing is to be something of a dialectic game, and the very first rule he registers is: "Try not only to silence, but to gain." This is hardly what we commonly think of as the scientific attitude.

On the whole, the notes which follow are of the type which these prefatory rules would lead one to expect: the logic is unimpeachable, but the premises and conclusions are unverified. Two of the most flagrant examples of this are the paragraphs on the influence of the stars in human affairs, and on the "Abyss." The first might well have been written by a medieval schoolman.

[Second Series] 32. To observe how the Planets may act on sublunary things, such as plants, animals, bodies of men, and indirectly upon their souls too, by that infinitely subtile matter diffused all around them; which, in all probability, is so subtile, as to permeate the Air, and any bodies whatsoever, but more especially the Moon, but most of all, the Comets, because of the great quantity that is diffused from them; and to show how it is probable, that the Ancients got the notion, from the long experience of the Antediluvians.

Just what he means by this last becomes clear in a later section of the notes, when he writes of the "effluvia of the planets," closing in this fashion:

It seems to me probable, that, before the Flood, when the Earth enjoyed so temperate and undisturbed an Atmosphere, when the effects of the stars, of this nature, were constant, being not disturbed by the perturbations of the Atmosphere, as now, and the lives of men were so long, that they knew the effects of the Planets upon the Earth; that they could foretell nearly what effect such a position or aspect of the Stars would produce in the Atmosphere, and upon the plants and animals of the Earth; having so much opportunity of experience and observation, by reason of their long lives; and that the tradition of this, from Noah and his sons to their

posterity, has been the cause of that general opinion, which the nations of the world have had, that the various phases and appearances of the plants had a considerable effect upon the earth; and thus gave rise to Judicial Astrology, and, in a great measure, to their Worshipping of the Planets.

This passage, with its amusing reasoning in a vacuum on unexamined premises, certainly cannot add much to Edwards' reputation as "a remarkable scientific observer."

In another section (number 71) we have an example of Edwards' treatment of facts when he found them blocking the course of his logic. This paragraph is labeled "Abyss," and begins with the assertion, made without proof, that "It is undoubted, that there is a vast Abyss of water under us, above which, the surface of the Earth is stretched forth, and on which it rests." Now, he proceeds, the water in the Abyss must be heavier than the matter of which the upper shell of the earth is composed in order to bear it up. On the other hand, the water of the Abyss must not be heavier by nature than the water on the surface of the earth, otherwise springs would be impossible. Therefore, he concludes, the greater specific gravity of the water of the Abyss must be due to its being compressed. So far his logic flows smoothly, but at this point Edwards bumps up against a scientific fact of his day; namely, that all experiments in compressing water had failed. He is conscious of this fact and states it, but instead of reëxamining his premises, he simply rests on the accuracy of his ratiocination, and calmly waves aside the findings of the laboratory with the remark that "if we cannot compress water . . . it is certainly merely for want of strength.". . .

There is no patient search for facts, indeed, as is revealed in his discussion of the abyss, hardly any patience with facts, when they oppose the flow of his reasoning. He was primarily a logician rather than a scientist.

In one very important passage in the notes on science he tells us what he is really driving at. In section 20 of "Things to be Considered" (second series) he makes a point, writes "Q. E. D.," at the conclusion of his argument, and then adds, "N. B. From this, again, to prove our whole scheme." Now what is it that Edwards asserts to be his "whole scheme" in the so-called "Notes on Natural Science"? The answer is obviously important, and in broad outline it is this: that matter is composed of indestructible units called atoms and that these atoms had to be created, aranged, and ordered by an Infinite, Omnipotent Power. That is "the whole scheme" of the "Notes on Natural Science." After a few preliminary propositions, he lays down "Proposition I," which is: "That All bodies whatsoever, except Atoms themselves, must, of absolute necessity, be composed of Atoms." He proves this by pointing out that unless a body were made of indestructible units, it could be annihilated by being pressed between two other objects. From this he proceeds to the assertion that if two atoms touch perfectly at their surfaces, they become one and cannot be separated any more than an atom itself can be divided. Therefore there must be an infinite power preserving atoms from destruction. Corollary three of this second proposition then is: "We have already as much as proved, that it is God himself, or the immediate exercise of his power, which keeps the parts of atoms . . . together." Corollary five reads: "Hence an incontestable argument for the being of a God." Corollaries six to fourteen follow the ramifications of this idea.

But, says Edwards, someone will object that in the constant jumbling together of atoms it is inevitable that sooner or later the surfaces of all atoms will accidentally make a perfect contact with the surfaces of all other atoms and so the universe becomes one indivisible lump. "I answer," writes Edwards in triumph, "I do not think it to be at all rash or absurd, to suppose, that the Almighty in the first creation, might take sufficient care to prevent any such fatal or inconvenient consequences, by creating the atoms, of which the Universe was to be composed, of such figures, as that no surface of any one should be suited to the surface of any other, as to be able to touch it by surfaces: which would prevent all that is objected." This can hardly be described as an "important first-hand observation in nature."

Time and again Edwards returns to this theme, the "whole scheme" of his notes: a metaphysical proof of the good Calvinistic doctrine of the sovereignty of God in terms of atoms. In section 88 he writes, "God designed the figure and shape of every atom, and likewise their places; which doubtless was done with infinite wisdom." In section 14 he records a resolution: "To show how the Motion, Rest, and Direction of the *Least Atom* has an influence on the motion, rest and direction of every body in the Universe" "motes, or straws and such little things, may be for some great uses in the whole course of things, throughout Eternity," that therefore "great wisdom . . . is necessary. . . . And then to show how God, who does this, must be necessarily *Omniscient*, and know every, the least thing, that must happen through

Eternity." The interest in theology in the notes on science is not merely incidental to the studies of nature; the whole scheme is fundamentally theological. The real interests and powers of Edwards are already evident in these records from his college days, and his final philosophy (perhaps one should say theology) had, in its general outlines, been adopted before his Senior year at Yale.

In discussing Edwards' defection in youth from the path which it is imagined he might have entered; namely science, much is made of his confession that from childhood his mind "had been full of objections against the doctrine of God's sovereignty," and that later he was converted to a glad acceptance of this dogma. Such a confession from a deeply conscientious and introspective Calvinist, looking back from pious heights upon his youth, must not be taken too literally. Vagrant thoughts, such as would inevitably come to a keen-minded boy, assume sinister shapes in the recollections of the devotee. There are many indications that in early youth Edwards entered the religious path, in which, barring minor deviations, consisting mainly in lapses from high seriousness, he walked to the grave. He recalls "seasons of awakening" experienced when he was only seven or eight years old. The tone in which he speaks of persons joining the church in a letter, written during such an "awakening" in his father's congregation when Edwards was thirteen, makes it appear that he was then already a member of the church himself. Dwight, who takes the great Calvinist's confession of youthful delinquency from faith very seriously, is worried by his inability to find "the precise period when he [Edwards] regarded himself as entering on

a religious life." "He no where mentions," continues Dwight; "nor have I found any record of the time, when he made a public confession of religion." The reason obviously is that Edwards joined the church very young, a not uncommon thing in that day, and hardly recollected a time when he was not committed to religion. Mr. Van Doren seems to think that the important moment was "On Saturday, 12 January, 1723," when, says Mr. Van Doren, "he made his solemn dedication," and quotes from Edwards' diary these words: "I have been before God, and have given myself, all that I am, and have, to God; so that I am not, in any respect, my own." Mr. Van Doren then comments, "He had taken the great step of his life; he had given up once for all the secular aspirations which might have hindered him in his career as the last High Priest of American Calvinism." The quotation above from Edwards' diary under the date January 12, 1723, upon which the assertion that this was the all-important day in Edwards' life rests, omits a very important sentence. Beside what has been quoted, Edwards wrote, "I have this day, solemnly renewed my baptismal covenant and self dedication, which I renewed when I was taken into the communion of the church." Edwards certainly did not feel that he had taken the "great step of his life." This was not a dedication, but a re-dedication; the vows which had been made at his baptism, and those which he had registered when he entered the church, were renewed. This was not an inauguration, but a step in his religious experience. He himself added in the diary for that day, "I gave myself to God in my baptism, and I have been this morning to him, and told him, that I gave myself *wholly* to him." He was not facing about, but simply taking another step in the direction in which he had walked since childhood. There never was a time when religion was not his primary concern.

There seems to have been a thin vein of scientific interest in the man, but, as Alexander V. G. Allen has put it, "Science and metaphysics do not interest him as ends in themselves, but as subordinated to a theological purpose. The God consciousness was the deepest substratum of his being, — his natural heritage from Puritan antecedents, coloring or qualifying every intellectual conviction he attained." He never formally renounced science, as he had never consciously espoused her. His lode of mysticism widened and deepened, in accordance with the promises of his youth. There are two types of mystics — the trite designations, radical and conservative, indicate their difference. In the one the

inner light burns so steadily and bravely that orthodoxies become insignificant; Luther and Roger Williams, not to mention Jesus, are examples. Of the other, and more common type, Newman is a representative. Mystics of this kind usually have a logical temper; they demand logical certainty, and so they rush into the solidest orthodoxy at hand, fearful that the least disturbance of their philosophic foundations will necessitate logical movements which will bring their mystical superstructure down in ruins. Edwards is distinctly of this latter type; he was rational but not adventurous. His whole life was marked by a gradual and logical hardening of his theological shell to protect the precious mystical flame within. That such a man was, or ever could have been, a "remarkable scientific observer" seems, despite his possession of some powers of observation, highly questionable.

Theodore Hornberger: EDWARDS A DISCIPLE OF NEWTON

Despite the doubts raised by Faust on his scientific achievements, Edwards did find Newton fascinating reading and he produced studies of unquestionable scientific import. Theodore Hornberger argues in the essay below that Newton's impact upon Edwards' thought and intellectual methods as evidenced in his scientific, philosophical and theological writings, was considerable. Edwards was as influenced as any of his contemporaries by the climate of thought created by Newtonian science, and perhaps with a greater degree of sophistication than any other colonial. Hornberger implies that the debate about Edwards' scientific achievements is colored too strongly by a modern distinction between science and religion which would not have occurred to either Newton or Edwards. In the eighteenth century, despite angry denunciations of religious superstition and obscurantism, many intellectuals believed science and religion reinforced and supported each other.

Theodore Hornberger, "The Effect of the New Science upon the Thought of Jonathan Edwards," *American Literature,* IX (November, 1937), pp. 196–207. Reprinted by permission of Duke University Press.

SOME YEARS ago, Mr. Clarence H. Faust reviewed in these pages the evidence of Jonathan Edwards's early interest in science, reaching the conclusion that from the first Edwards's powers were dedicated to theology rather than to science. No quarrel with this judgment is intended in the present article, which seeks rather to present proof that Edwards's metaphysics, and hence his theology, were markedly influenced by the new science, however subordinate science may have been in the mind of the theologian. The suggestion of such influence is not new, but heretofore, so far as is known to the present writer, no one has troubled to demonstrate it, even though it appears to be the thread that unravels much that is difficult to understand in Edwards's intellectual outlook.

The constant factor in Edwards's thinking is probably, as most commentators say, subjective idealism, whether derived from someone like Berkeley or arrived at independently. That philosophy was in the air when Edwards was a youth, and it was attractive to the theologically-minded because it appeared to be a great support to religion. Berkeley, we are told, developed his metaphysics for fear and hate of the materialistic tendencies of the followers of Locke and Newton; Edwards's famous essay "Of Being" concludes with the statement that "those who think material things the most substantial beings, and spirits more like a shadow" are making a "gross mistake." The same essay asserts without equivocation that "Space is God," and that the universe "exists no where, but in the Divine mind." These are concepts so similar to those of Malebranche, Norris, and Berkeley that it is fairly safe to conclude that Edwards, like those philosophers, was primarily anxious to save God and spirit and religion from the scientific glorification of matter.

It is significant that the essay "Of Being" was a part of the manuscript "Notes on Natural Science," begun, together with the parallel notes on "The Mind," when Edwards was an undergraduate. These notebooks reveal much speculation that is scientific in spirit, from the rule: "Always, when I have occasion, to make use of mathematical proofs," to the assertion that the principles laid down in the essay, "Of Being," do not "make void Natural Philosophy, or the science of the Causes or Reasons of corporeal changes; For to find out the reasons of things in Natural Philosophy, is only to find out the proportion of God's acting." There are many notes, moreover, called "things to be considered, or written fully about," which show Edwards's wide though somewhat uneven reading in the sciences. In optics and astronomy, particularly, he was much interested, and his comments indicate his awareness of important problems in these fields. In other subjects, such as physiology and geology, he was still using the dialect of the ancient and medieval philosophers. Some of the things he set down for consideration were these:

11. To show, from Sir Isaac Newton's principles of light and colours, why the sky is blue; . . . why the Sun is yellow, when rising and setting, and sometimes, in smoky weather, of a blood red; why the Clouds, and the Atmosphere, near the horizon, appear red and yellow, before sun-rising, and after sun-setting; why distant Mountains are blue, etc.

4. To know the shape of the Spheroid of the Universe, by observation of the Milky Way; and to know whereabout our System is in it; 1st, with respect to the plane of the greatest circles, from observations of the ratio of the brightness of the opposite sides

compounded with several other ratios. — 2d. With respect to the latitude, or the axis of this Spheroid, by observing how much the Milky Way differs from a great circle. . . .

It is not probable that, when the parts of the body are touched, the Animal Spirits, that were in those parts of the nerves, go quite to the brain before the soul perceives, but that motion is continued to the brain, in the tubes that contain the animal spirits, as motion in a tube filled with water. If the water at one end moves never so little, the motion is continued quite to the other end; or as the motion, given to the blood in the Arteries, by the pulse of the heart, is communicated all over the body. . . .

45. To observe, it is somewhat difficult to know, how it comes to pass, that there are, in all Continents, however uneven and confused, hilly and jumbled, though they seem to have mountains and vallies, indifferently, and undesignedly, every where dispersed; yet, that there are such convenient Channels, whereby water may be conveyed from the middle of the Continents, and from all parts, into the Ocean. The reason is, when the world was first created, the water covering all the earth, the surface of the earth must needs be very soft, and loose, and easily worn or altered, by the motions of the water; and afterwards, the water, retiring in such a vast body, into one place, from off the continents, and some places of the continents, being higher, and others lower, some were easily worn, others more difficult; in some places, the waters moving with more force, in others with less, some places would necessarily be worn deeper than others, from the middle of the continent to the ocean; and as the water decreased, as going off from the earth, all would retire into those channels: and, the water still decreasing, the remainder would run in the deeper places of these channels; and after they (the waters) were gone, they left channels everywhere; into which, the waters afterwards gushing out, in various parts of the continent, would naturally find their way: Thus, also, after the Deluge, when the surface of the earth was again loosened.

Thus Edwards turned occasionally to scientific hypotheses, and even, more rarely, to direct observation and experiment. Even in these college notes, however, the dominant tone is the theological, and the more typical comments are such as these:

To show how Infinite Wisdom must be exercised, in order that *Gravity* and *Motion* may be perfectly harmonious; and that, although the jumble of the Epicureans be allowed, although it be, in fact, impossible. . . .

To bring in an observation, somewhere in the proper place, that — instead of Hobbes' notion, that God is matter, and that all substance is matter — that nothing, that is matter, can possibly be God; and that no matter is, in the most proper sense, matter, . . .

To observe that, if bodies have no substance of their own, so neither is solidity, strictly speaking, a property belonging to body, and to show how. And if solidity is not so, neither are the other properties of body, which depend upon it, and are only modifications of it; so that there is neither real substance, nor property, belonging to bodies; but all that is real is immediately in the First Being. *Coroll.* 1. Hence see how God is said, still more properly, to be *Ens entium,* or, if there was nothing else in the world but bodies, the only *Real Thing,* so that it may be said, in a stricter sense than hitherto, "Thou art, and there is none beside thee." *Coroll.* 2. Hence see, that, instead of Matter being the only proper substance, and more substantial than any thing else, because it is hard and solid; yet, it is truly nothing at all, strictly and in itself considered. *Coroll.* 3. The nearer in nature beings are to God, so much the more properly are they *beings,* and more substantial. And that Spirits are much more properly beings, and more substantial, than bodies.

Such statements leave no room for doubt of the centrality of subjective idealism in Edwards's thinking, nor of the share of the new science in pushing him to that position. His mention of the Epicureans and of Thomas Hobbes is enough to show his fear of the materialistic implications of seventeenth-century scientific thought. It is evident that Edwards, like the other idealists of his time, was deriving from science itself a new metaphysics, and a metaphysics which permitted more fully even than Newton's the retention of God in the world. By the time he had finished college in 1720, science would seem to have definitely affected Edwards's idea of God. It was not the only influence upon his thinking, to be sure; as one of his biographers says, he had reached a conclusion, "driven thereto by the threefold suggestions of physics — God is space; of philosophy — God is mind; and of religious experience — God is the source of our intuitions." There is every reason to believe that Edwards had reached this conclusion before he left college, and that it persisted throughout the remainder of his life, coloring his utterances upon almost every subject that he touched.

Before turning to his writings, we should note that his reading list is added evidence of a mild but lifelong interest in science and particularly in the writings of Newton. His reasons for that interest, and his own peculiar subordination of science to religion, may best be seen, however, in his printed books.

After leaving college, Edwards studied theology, preached for short periods in New York and Connecticut, and served for two years as a tutor at Yale. Not until 1727 was he ordained at Northampton; not until 1731 did he publish his first sermon, *God Glorified in the Work of Redemption, by the Greatness of Man's Dependence upon Him* (Boston, 1731). In this and in his second printed sermon, *A Divine and Supernatural Light Shown to Be Both a Scriptural and a Rational Doctrine* (Boston, 1734), may be seen the first expression of the new religious vigor which was Edwards's chief contribution to New England life.

He who reads these sermons today feels, as the average listener probably did in the 1730's, that there is no great break between Edwards and his predecessors. The Mathers, for instance, speak in the same dialect of the glory of God and the power of His will. On closer examination, however, a difference appears which may in part be accounted for by perceiving it as an extension of scientific and philosophical speculations. As A. V. G. Allen puts it, at a time "when the prevailing Deism represented God as if a passive agent, governing the world by general laws and second causes, as well as far removed from the scene of human activity, Edwards presented Deity as immanent and efficient will." In his earlier thinking Edwards had conceived of God as underlying all external phenomena. "It was God's immediate action on the mind, in accordance with His fixed and stable will, which gives to the mind the idea of an external world." He now, as Allen suggests, extends this conception to the world within. "In the invisible sphere of man's moral or intellectual existence, God was still the universal substance; it was he alone that existed and there is none else." Looking at it from this angle, it becomes reasonable to believe that much of Edwards's theological importance comes as a result of this extension to the moral sphere of his scientific and philosophical conceptions. He gave to the old Calvinism a new idea of God.

This new synthesis of science, philosophy, and theology doubtless justified to Edwards his stirring and epoch-making preaching of the all-importance of God and the insignificance of humanity. It cannot be said, however, that his new concept of Deity shines clearly through his works, and it is probable that the majority of his hearers interpreted his words in terms of the old transcendent, anthropomorphic Deity of the Old Testament. Nor did Edwards shake himself entirely free of that conception, as may be seen in the famous Enfield sermon *Sinners in the Hands of an Angry God* (Boston, 1741), or in his posthumous *History of the Work of Redemption* (Edinburgh, 1774), in both of which God is anything but immanent will. Throughout his life, as Professor McGiffert says, Edwards's mind passed "back and forth with no apparent jolt or difficulty from a pantheistic to a personalistic interpretation of God.... It seems not to have dawned on him that there is a contradiction in speaking of God as at the same time a person and an expansive substance."

Despite his idealistic world-view, therefore, Edwards did not hesitate to make use of the familiar analogies and dialectic of Calvinism; and the great part of his work appears to the average reader to be entirely theological, utterly untouched by any speculation outside of Scriptural exegesis. In his significant relation to the Great Awakening, for example, there is no noticeable evidence that clearly indicates anything but a transcendent and personal Deity. His many writings about the phenomena of conversion, so interesting to the student of the psychology of religion, show no particular effect of scientific thought. The same thing may be justly said of his many sermons, which are singularly free of allusions or arguments based

either upon science or upon his philosophical speculations. For the evidence that he returned to science and philosophy, we must go to the great theological works of his last years, written in exile at Stockbridge.

The first of these, *A Careful and Strict Enquiry into the Modern Prevailing Notions of Freedom of the Will* (Boston, 1754), is concerned with an old theological problem reinvigorated by the Deistic controversy. As Paul Elmer More states it, Edwards's book represents the Calvinist angle of a triangular controversy with the Deists and the Arminians over the place of evil in the universe. At first glance nothing would seem to be further from the realm of science. One needs, however, to follow only a little of the knotty argument of the *Freedom of the Will* to perceive that the book is saturated with the effects of science. Full quotation would require many pages, but it could reasonably support the argument that Edwards's definition of cause and his discussion of causation, as well as his vigorous defense of moral necessity, depend in great measure upon illustrations and reasoning drawn from the new science. One example must suffice. A stock Arminian argument against Calvinistic determinism had been that God could hardly be concerned with the innumerable minute differences visible in the world. "To which I answer," says Edwards, in a passage which exhibits both his science and his inexorable logic:

it is impossible for us to determine, with any certainty or evidence, that because the difference is very small, and appears to us of no consideration, therefore there is absolutely no superior goodness, and no valuable end, which can be proposed by the Creator and Governor of the world, in ordering such a difference. The forementioned author mentions many instances. One is, there being one atom in the whole universe, more or less. . . . It is possible that the most minute effects of the Creator's power, the smallest assignable difference between the things which God has made, may be attended, in the whole series of events, and the whole compass and extent of their influence, with very great and important consequences. If the laws of motion and gravitation, laid down by Sir Isaac Newton, hold universally, there is not one atom, nor the least assignable part of an atom, but what has influence every moment throughout the whole material universe, to cause every part to be otherwise than it would be if it were not for that particular corporeal existence. And however the effect is insensible for the present, yet it may, in length of time, become great and important. To illustrate this, let us suppose two bodies moving the same way, in straight lines, perfectly parallel one to another; but to be diverted from this parallel course, and drawn one from another, as much as might be by the attraction of an atom, at the distance of one of the furthest of the fixed stars from the earth; these bodies being turned out of the lines of their parallel motion, will, by degrees, get further and further distant, one from the other; and though the distance may be imperceptible for a long time, yet at length it may become very great. So the revolution of a planet round the sun being retarded or accelerated, and the orbit of its revolution made greater or less, and more or less elliptical, and so its periodical time longer or shorter, no more than may be by the influence of the least atom, might, in length of time, perform a whole revolution sooner or later than otherwise it would have done; which might make a vast alteration with regard to millions of important events. So the influence of the least particle may, for aught we know, have such effect on something in the constitution of some human body, as to cause another thought to arise in the mind at a certain time, than otherwise would have been; which, in length of time (yea, and that not very great) might occasion a vast alteration through the whole world of mankind. And so innumerable other ways might be mentioned, wherein the least assignable alteration may possibly be attended with great consequences.

So frequent are such analogies and illustrations from science, and particularly from physics and astronomy, that one might almost argue from Edwards's writings that he believed in an uninterrupted order of nature. However, he concludes the *Freedom of the Will* with a view of providence which leaves room for divine interposition.

Equally impregnated with the effects of science is Edwards's *Great Christian Doctrine of Original Sin Defended* (Boston, 1758), a book not yet off the press when he died. One passage in it particularly exemplifies the close relation of his theological ideas regarding the intellectual and moral world to his scientific notions. He is writing about his belief that a tendency to evil exists in the very nature of mankind. In all colonial literature there is perhaps no more acute analysis of the scientific method:

The natural dictate of reason shews that where there is an effect there is a cause, and a cause sufficient for the effect; because if it were not sufficient, it would not be effectual; and that therefore, where there is a stated prevalence of the effect, there is a stated prevalence in the cause. A steady effect argues a steady cause. We obtain a notion of tendency, no other way than by observation: And we can observe nothing but events: And it is the commonness or constancy of events that gives us a notion of tendency in all cases. Thus we judge of tendencies in the natural world. Thus we judge of the tendencies or propensities of nature in minerals, vegetables, animals, rational and irrational creatures. A notion of a stated tendency or fixed propensity, is not obtained by observing only a single event. A stated preponderation in the cause or occasion, is argued only by a stated prevalence of the effect. If a die be once thrown and it falls on a particular side, we do not argue from hence, that *that* side is the heaviest; but if it be thrown without skill or care many thousands or millions of times, and it constantly falls on the same side, we have not the least doubt in our minds but that there is something of propensity in the case, by superior weight of that side, or in some other respect. How ridiculous would he make himself, who should earnestly dispute against any tendency in the state of things to cold in the winter or heat in the summer; or should stand to it, that although it often happened that water quenched fire, yet there was no tendency in it to such an effect?

That we are dealing with human nature does not alter the case, continues Edwards; "the evidence of tendency" remains the same. If there were a particular family

which, from generation to generation, and through every remove to innumerable different countries and places of abode, all died of a consumption, or all run distracted, or all murdered themselves, it would be as much an evidence of the *tendency* of something in the nature or constitution of that *race*, as it would be of the tendency of something in the nature or state of an individual, if some one person had lived all that time, and some remarkable event had often appeared in him, which he had been the agent or subject of from year to year and age to age, continually and without fail.

In such comments as these there is abundant evidence that Edwards possessed in a degree uncommon to his age the scientific mind, which seeks always to relate particular events to general laws.

The work which sums up Edwards's cosmology, however, is his *Dissertation Concerning the End for Which God Created the World* (Boston, 1765). Competent scholars have regarded this as his most important work, and there is reason to believe that it contains his most mature opinion of a subject which he regarded as of extreme importance. We at once face the question, therefore, of the relation of science to this final statement of his theology.

Let it be said, first of all, that the thought in this dissertation on God's end in creation marks a return (or, as some think, a development) of Edwards's early idealism. He begins with God, the eternal and infinite Being, Who, he says, "is in effect, *Being in general;* and comprehends universal existence." Although his terminology is difficult, and he is not always clear, he appears to most readers to vacillate between an anthropomorphic God the Creator, and a concept expressed by "emanation," which suggests the idea of God as universal substance. Our question becomes, consequently, that of the relation of science to Edward's idealism.

Let us bring in for purposes of comparison another New England book, John Cotton's *Briefe Exposition upon Ecclesiastes* (London, 1654). Like Edwards's *Dissertation*, Cotton's book insists upon the glory of God and the insufficiency of the creature in the attainment of true happiness. Cotton's exegesis of the "Vanity of vanities; all is vanity" chapter demonstrates the unprofitableness of the study of nature as compared to the contemplation of God; Edwards states that "the whole system of created beings, in comparison of the Creator, would be found as the light dust of the balance, or even as nothing and vanity." And yet, despite their agreement on this point, what a vast difference there is between these two books! The material world seemed to Cotton a neat mixture of the four elements, with the earth firmly occupying the central position in the universe, demonstrating to man the transitory quality of his own life and the permanence of the creation. The material world seemed to Edwards to have real existence only in terms of mind or divine idea, although for practical purposes it could be conceived of as composed of innumerable dissimilar particles held together by the God-revealing law of universal attraction; the earth and the solar system were to him but one of the innumerable manifestations of the Deity, demonstrating chiefly the dominance of mind or spirit in the universe. Cotton and Edwards, in other words, although both Calvinists, held quite distinct metaphysical beliefs, and differed widely in their concepts of Deity.

There is perhaps no way of direct proof that these differences were the effect of the advance of science, but the presumption that they were is almost irresistible.

One need but note that Edwards's immanency permits a far more sophisticated idea of God, and leaves room for uninterrupted causation or, better yet, one need but try to conceive of Edwards's having reached the position he did without the work of Locke and Newton, to realize that there is some relation, and probably a rather close one, between science and this reinterpretation of Calvinist theology. Edwards, as much as Berkeley, is best understood as a theological product of reaction against the materialistic aspects of seventeenth-century science.

Philosophically speaking, there are inconsistencies in Edwards's position of which he seems not to have been aware. He postulates, for instance, an infinite and eternal Deity, Who is, in effect, Being in general, suggesting that all substance is in some degree emanation of the Deity. Yet he is anxious, in his early notes on natural science, to deny an infinite universe, and insists in one of his sermons that "there is a certain place, a

particular part of the external creation, to which Christ is gone, and where he remains. And this place is that which we call the highest heaven, or the heaven of heavens; a place beyond all the visible heavens." Likewise, from a theological standpoint, his suggestion that the creation is an emanation of the infinite and eternal Deity is contradicted by his insistence on finite and temporal bounds to that creation.

These inconsistencies do not detract, however, from Edwards's achievement. His effect upon the religious life of the American people and upon the theological school which followed in his footsteps can hardly be exaggerated. Through all his works, Allen says, there runs the common purpose of bringing back the world again to God, and in that purpose he succeeded far beyond what might have been expected. Not only is he the key to the characteristic American confidence in revivalism, but in theology, we are told, he was "the chief human instrument in turning back the current for over a century in the larger part of New England to the theory of salvation and of man's dependence on God which marked the earlier types of Calvinism."

Edwards, in brief, accomplished what Samuel Johnson, Berkeley's disciple, failed to do. He succeeded in turning back for a large number of Americans and over a considerable length of time the tide of materialism to which the new science in some measure contributed. And Edwards accomplished this pious work not by attacking science, as Johnson and the Hutchinsonians tended to do, but by utilizing it, by implicit confidence that the study of natural things is "the discovery of the proportion of God's acting." From the new science, among other things, he developed a new foundation for his burning and mystical worship of God.

IV. JONATHAN EDWARDS AS A CRITIC OF THE ENLIGHTENMENT

John Taylor: ORIGINAL SIN IS AN IMMORAL AND UNREASONABLE DOCTRINE

John Taylor (1694–1761) was a nonconforming English divine and Hebrew scholar. His philosophical and religious beliefs reflected a trend in the Age of Reason towards a strictly rational and benevolent Christianity, partly in reaction to the rigors of Calvinism. Taylor went so far as to question the divinity of Christ and the morality of the doctrine of original sin. He scandalized many contemporaries by saying that both were unnecessary. His work on original sin was published in 1738 and became widely influential in England, Scotland and America. In it Taylor took an "Arminian" view of human self-reliance which Edwards believed was most destructive to Christianity. In the following selection, Taylor attacks any notion that man is a totally corrupt and helpless sinner, and instead he praises man as God's greatest creation. Man is freely endowed with powers of reason and moral goodness which would raise him to sublime heights. God, too, is portrayed as benevolent and primarily concerned with human happiness. Despite Edwards' criticism, Taylor's views received widespread interest in America, and his writings substantially assisted the emergence of liberal religion in late eighteenth-century colonial life.

THAT WE are born into the world capable of sin and wickedness is true; and that our constitution is attended with many sensual appetites and passions, which if excessive or irregular, become sinful, is also true; and that there is danger, great danger, of their becoming excessive and irregular in a world so corrupt and full of temptation as ours is, is also true. But all this does not amount to a *natural propensity* to sin. For, I presume, by a natural propensity, is meant, a necessary inclination to sin, or that we are necessarily sinful from the original bent and bias of our natural powers; which must be false. For

then we should not be sinful at all: because that which is necessary, or which we cannot help, is not sin. That we are weak and liable to temptation is the will of God, holy and good, and for glorious purposes to ourselves: but if we are wicked, it must be our own fault, and cannot proceed from any constraint, or necessity in our constitution.

For as to any moral taint or infection derived from Adam, give me leave honestly to confess, I do not understand what can be meant by it in any consistency with sense or truth. I do not know that we derive anything at all from Adam, but by the will and operation of

From John Taylor, *The Scripture-Doctrine of Original Sin proposed to Free and Candid Examination* (2nd ed. London: M. Fenner, 1741), pp. 186–188, 232–234, 256–262. In "Supplement," pp. 108–109, 140–143, 146–147.

God, no more than the acorn derives from the oak. It is, I judge, a great, though common fallacy, to suppose that something is infused into the human nature, some quality or other, not from the choice of our own minds, but like a taint, tincture, or infection, altering the natural constitutions, faculties and dispositions of our souls, absolutely independent of ourselves, and not from the will of God. That this taint runs like a stream from generation to generation, and is transmitted among ourselves from one to another, while God looks on, sees the thing done, and hates and curses us for it. Which supposes that He has no hand in it, (for how could he hate us for it, if it were of his own doing?) and yet, on the other hand, all sides allow that it is what we can neither help nor hinder, and consequently cannot be our fault: and then how can it be a moral taint or corruption? Can there be any moral corruption in us, which we neither can, nor ever could help or hinder? which is not our fault? Surely it is quite impossible, and directly repugnant to the nature of things. For nature cannot be morally corrupted, but by the will, the depraved choice of a moral agent: neither can any corrupt my nature, or make me wicked, but I myself.

* * *

We are born into the world quite ignorant, *Job* xi. 12. Vain man would be wise, though man be born like a wild ass's colt. We are born as void of actual knowledge as the brutes themselves. We are born with many sensual appetites, and consequently liable to temptation and sin. But this is not the fault of our nature, but the will of God, wise and good. For every one of our natural passions and appetites are in themselves good; of great use and advantage in our present circumstances: and our nature would be defective, sluggish or unarmed, without them. Nor is there any one of them we can at present spare. Our passions and appetites are in themselves, wisely, and kindly too, implanted in our nature, and become evil only by unnatural excess, or wicked abuse. The possibility of which excess and abuse is also well and wisely permitted for our trial. For without some such appetites, our reason would have nothing to struggle with, and consequently our virtue could not be duly exercised and proved in order to its being rewarded. And the appetites we have God has judged most proper, both for our use and trial.

On the other hand, we are born with rational powers, which gradually, and as God has been pleased to appoint, do grow up into a capacity of the most useful knowledge, though of different degrees. Even the heathen (*Rom.* i. 20, 21) knew God, and might have glorified him as God. But under the glorious light of the Gospel, we have very clear ideas of the divine perfections, and particularly of the love of God, as our Father, and as the God and Father of our Lord and Saviour Jesus Christ; we see our duty in the utmost extent, and the most cogent reasons to perform it; we have eternity opened to us, even an endless state of honour and felicity, the reward of virtuous actions, and the Spirit of God promised for our direction and assistance. And all this may and ought to be applied to the purifying of our minds, and the perfecting of holiness. To this light, and to these happy advantages we are born; for which we are bound for ever to praise and magnify the rich grace of God in the Redeemer. And all men in the world are born to some light, and some advantages, for which they are accountable; though only according to the several degrees of their light and advantages.

This idea then we ought to have of our being: that every thing in it is formed and appointed just as it should be: that it is a noble and invaluable gift bestowed upon us by the bounty of God, with which we should be greatly pleased, and for which we should be continually and heartily thankful: that it is a perishable thing, which needs to be diligently guarded, and cultivated: that our sensual inclinations are to be duly restrained and disciplined, and our rational powers faithfully applied to their proper uses: that God has given us those rational powers attended with those sensual inclinations, as for other good purposes, so in particular to try us, whether we will carefully guard and look after this most invaluable gift of his goodness: and that if we do not, he will in justice punish our wicked contempt of his love; but if we do, he will graciously reward our wisdom and virtue. And all, and every one of these considerations should be a spur to our diligence, and animate our endeavours to answer these most high and most excellent purposes of his wisdom and goodness.

* * *

Is it not highly injurious to the God of our nature, whose hands have fashioned and formed us, to believe our nature is originally corrupted, and in the worst sense of corruption too? And are not such doctrines, (which represent the divine dispensations as unjust, cruel and tyrannical) the source of those gloomy and blasphemous thoughts that infest and distract many good and honest souls? For I am apt to think common experience will make it good, that the more any study, and persuade themselves of the truth of such points, the more they are liable to dreadful, terrifying apprehensions of the deity, and the most ugly thoughts and injections.

I am ready to make all proper allowance for the prejudices of education: but is it fair and fitting, can it be pleasing to God, to look only at the imperfections of our being? Is it not impious falsely and unreasonably to magnify them, while we overlook, or but little regard, our blessings and advantages? Is this the way to give glory to God, our good and wise Maker? to increase our thankfulness, or to excite to proper diligence in improving the noble gifts he has bestowed upon us? Rather, is it not to pick quarrels with his work, and to disparage his gifts? Has it not a tendency to chill and benumb our spirits, to cool our love, to damp holy joy and praise, which should be the life of a Christian, and to cut the sinews of cheerful endeavours? No wonder we creep on in our Christian course half desponding, when our hearts are clogged with such weights as these? Is this our kindness and love to him that made us? Do we thus requite our Father by running down and lessening his beneficence? To disparage our nature, is to disparage the works and gifts of God.

Does not the doctrine of original sin teach you to transfer your wickedness and sin to a wrong cause? Whereas in truth you ought to blame or condemn yourself alone for any wicked lusts, which prevail in your heart, any evil habits you have contracted, any sinful actions you commit, you lay the whole upon Adam. Adam, you say, is the cause of the corruption of your nature, and the corruption of your nature is the cause of all your actual transgressions in thought, word and deed. — The world is very corrupt, and you are more or less stained with the pollution. True: but you refer it to a wrong cause, and such a cause as makes it cease to be corruption, or really charges God with it. And what good end do you promote by this? Humiliation and repentence? No. Cheerful obedience? No. The love of God? No. No, but you embarrass, perplex and hinder all these virtues, and all other religious duties.

What can be more destructive of virtue than to have a notion that you must, in some degree or other, be necessarily vicious? And has not the common doctrine of original sin a manifest tendency to propagate such a notion? And is it not to be feared so many children of good parents have degenerated because in the forms of religious instruction they have imbibed ill principles, and such as really are contrary to holiness? For to represent sin as natural, as altogether unavoidable, is to embolden in sin, and to give not only an excuse, but a reason for sinning.

If we believe we are in nature worse than the brutes, and this doctrine represents us as such, what wonder if we act worse than brutes? The generality of Christians have embraced this persuasion. And what wonder if the generality of Christians have been the most wicked, lewd, bloody, and treacherous of all mankind? Certainly nothing generous, great, good, pure can spring from principles, to say the least, so low and groveling.

It is matter of great admiration, that the Christian religion, which is calculated and intended to raise our hearts above the riches and splendor of the world, and to teach us self-denial, humility, love, goodness, innocence, etc. should be perverted to the vile purposes of temporal wealth, power, pride, malice and cruelty. And to me it is no less surprising, that whereas the Christian religion is wonderfully adapted to inspire the most pleasing and joyful sentiments of the divine goodness and love, the Gospel has been so far turned the wrong way, that Christians have lost even a sense of the beneficence of God in giving them a rational nature; and are so far from rendering the praise of this his first and original liberality, that it is the common persuasion of every Christian, that he ought, all the days of his life, to look upon his nature with abhorrence; and, instead of being thankful, to be humbled for it. Which is to abhor and be humbled for the munificence of his maker. For certainly the nature of every man that comes into the world, and as he comes into the world, can be no other than the work and gift of God. This, I confess, seems to me a master-piece of the old serpent's subtilty, who has been for a long time let loose to deceive the nations. *Rev.* xx. 3.

Must it not greatly sink the credibility of the Gospel to suppose it teaches the common doctrine of original sin? For if it is easily seen to be an absurdity, who can believe that to be a revelation from God which is chargeable with it? And I make no doubt this, with other pretended principles of the like nature, have filled our land with infidels. Such doctrines set religion in direct opposition to reason and common sense, and so render our rational powers quite useless to us, and consequently religion too. For a religion which we cannot understand, or which is not the object of a rational belief, is no religion for reasonable beings.

Is not this doctrine hurtful to the power of godliness, not only as it fills men's heads with frightful chimeras, and loads their consciences with the heaviest fetters of error, but also as it diverts their thoughts from the heavenly and substantial truths of religion? as it throws the method and means of our salvation into perplexity and confusion, and renders all religious principles uncertain? We are made sinners we know not how, and therefore must be sorry for, and repent of, we know not what. We are made sinners in an arbitrary way, and we are made saints in an arbitrary way. But what is arbitrary can be brought under no rules.

Which notions are most likely to operate best upon parents' minds, and most proper to be instilled into a child? That it is born a child of wrath, that it comes into the world under God's curse, that its being, as soon as given, is in the worst and most deplorable state of corruption? Or, that it is born under the smiles of heaven, endowed with noble capacities, and formed in love, for the glory of God and its own happiness, if his goodness is not despised and neglected?

Must it not lessen the due love of parents to children, to believe they are the vilest and most wretched creatures in the world, the objects of God's wrath and curse? And what encouragement have they to bring them up in the nurture and admonition of the Lord, if they think they are under the certain curse of God to eternal damnation, and but under a very uncertain hope of his blessing and favor?

Young people are exhorted to remember their creator: but how can they remember him without the utmost horror, who, it is supposed, has given them life under such deplorable circumstances?

* * *

And if God creates the nature of every man in the womb, he must create it with all the properties and qualities which belong to that nature as it is then, and so made. For it is impossible God should make our nature, and yet not make the qualities which it has when made; because this would be at the same time to make it what it is and what it is not. No substance can be made without some qualities and properties belonging to it. And it must necessarily, so soon as it is made, have those qualities which the maker gives it, and no other: for should it, in the very instant it is made, and as it comes out of his hands, have any other, then it would at the same time both be and not be what he has made it.

And if God creates the nature of every individual person in the womb with all its properties and qualities, then whatever those properties and qualities are, whether bodily infirmities, or any particular passions, appetites, principles, propensities, dispositions, etc. such qualities must necessarily be the will and work of God, and such as he in his infinite wisdom judges fit and expedient to belong to the nature of every individual. For out of his hands alone the nature of every man in the world doth, and must necessarily come attended with those qualities which God gives it, and no other.

Consequently, those passions, appetites, propensities, etc. cannot be sinful in us; because they are, and can be no other than the will and work of God in us. If there are ferments in our flesh and blood, or any principles and seeds in any part of our constitution, as soon as formed in the womb, those ferments cannot be vicious, nor the ferments of spite and envy as they are then and there in our nature; nor can those principles be principles of iniquity, nor those seeds the seeds of sin, as then planted in our constitution, because they are all then and there formed, infused, and planted by the hand of our good and holy Creator. They are indeed such passions, propensities, appetites, ferments, etc. as may be viciously and sinfully applied; but they cannot be vicious and sinful in themselves, nor as originally belonging to our constitution. Because as they are originally in our constitution, they can be no other than the workmanship of God; and moreover there is not one of them that can be named, but may be applied to virtuous as well as vicious purposes.

But if divines will say, that such passions, appetites, propensities are sinful, and render us the objects of God's wrath and displeasure; they should consider, it is infinitely absurd, and highly dishonorable to God to suppose he is displeased at us, and regards us as the objects of his wrath for what he himself has infused into our nature. For it is evident beyond all contradiction, that, if those passions and propensities are sinful, the sinfulness of them is not in any equity or justice to be charged upon me, or upon my nature; nor in any fair or upright dealing can I be under the wrath or displeasure of God for them, unless that can be sinful or deserving of wrath in me, which is neither caused, advised, nor consented to by me, or unless I can deserve God's wrath and displeasure, because I was over-powered when I could not possibly resist: or unless it be displeasing to God for no power to be overcome by his own almighty power. This argument will also hold good with regard to any other power, or virtue which may, though absurdly, be supposed to give us our natural qualities, etc. For in this case they would not be sinful in us; because infused into us by a power under which we were altogether passive, and to which we had no power to oppose. In both cases sinfulness will be natural, that is to say, necessary and unavoidable to us; and if so, then no sinfulness with regard to us; for nothing can be sinful in me which I can no ways avoid, help or hinder.

* * *

The great, the wise and good God gives every man what particular passions and appetites, and in what degree he thinks fit, and adjusts every man's trial as to kind and circumstances no doubt in perfect equity and goodness. He, with his own hand measures to every man his capacities, talents, means, and opportunities. We are born neither righteous nor sinful; but capable of being either, as we improve or neglect the goodness of God, who sends every man into the world under his blessing; endows every man with that sense of truth and falsehood, right and wrong, which we call conscience, to be an intimate monitor and guide at all times. He affords every man sufficient light to know his duty, and has set before him many motives to perform it; he allows every man the benefit of repentance and pardon if he transgresses; and at the last day will in perfect equity judge every man according to his particular case and situation in life. Thus God has made every one of us a present of a rational being, the noblest and most invaluable gift, upon the most reasonable and beneficent terms, and for the highest and most glorious end, viz. that being cultivated and seasoned with the habits of virtue in our present state of probation, it may be exalted to immortal honor and glory in the future world. And this gift we should highly prize, thankfully accept from the kind and bountiful donor, and instead of finding fault with it, and his dispensations, should magnify his goodness, and apply ourselves vigorously to improve our being, and to comply with the discipline he has prescribed, in hopes of the glory he has promised; being persuaded, that the Lord is righteous in all his ways, and holy in all his words; and that if we fail of attaining the perfections and happiness of the future world, it will one day be made to appear before angels and men to be our own very great fault, and not the fault of our nature, or the munificent donor of it, the Father of our spirits, to whom be glory and honor for ever.

Jonathan Edwards: ATTACK AGAINST TAYLOR'S VIEW OF ORIGINAL SIN

Taylor's Original Sin *aroused a stormy controversy. In England Isaac Watts and John Wesley considered Taylor's position dangerously subversive because it gave too small a place to God's grace in the conversion of men. In Massachusetts the debate was no less lively. Edwards entered the fray in a direct attack upon Taylor, publishing what he considered one of his most important treatises. Edwards meant* The Great Christian Doctrine of Original Sin Defended *(1757) to be his definitive statement against the growing popularity of liberal humanistic religion. To him, the doctrine of original sin, and its corollary, total depravity, was true according to revelation, metaphysics and the facts of human experience.*

THE QUESTION to be considered, in order to determine whether man's nature is not *depraved and ruined,* is not, whether he is not inclined to perform as many *good deeds* as *bad ones;* but which of these two he preponderates to, in the frame of his heart, and state of his nature, *a state of innocence and righteousness, and favor with God; or a state of sin, guiltiness, and abhorrence in the sight of God.* Persevering sinless righteousness, or else the guilt of sin, is the alternative, on the decision of which depends (as is confessed), according to the nature and truth of things, as they are in themselves, and according to the rule of right, and of perfect justice, man's being approved and accepted of his Maker, and eternally blessed as good; or his being rejected, thrown away, and cursed as bad. And therefore the determination of the tendency of man's heart and nature, with respect to these terms, is that which is to be looked at, in order to determine whether his nature is good or evil, pure or corrupt, sound or ruined. If such be man's nature, and state of his heart, that he has an infallibly effectual propensity to the latter of those terms; then it is wholly impertinent to talk of *the innocent and kind actions, even of criminals themselves, surpassing their crimes in numbers, and of the prevailing innocence, good nature, industry, felicity, and cheerfulness of the greater part of mankind.* Let never so many thousands or millions of acts of honesty, good nature, &c., be supposed; yet, by the supposition, there is an unfailing propensity to such moral evil, as in its dreadful consequences infinitely outweighs all effects or consequences of any supposed good.

From Jonathan Edwards, *The Works of President Edwards,* vol. II, pp. 322–325, 330–332, 339.

Surely that tendency, which, in effect, is an infallible tendency to eternal destruction, is an infinitely dreadful and pernicious tendency; and that nature and frame of mind, which implies such a tendency, must be an infinitely dreadful and pernicious frame of mind. It would be much more absurd to suppose that such a state of nature is good, or not bad, under a notion of men's doing more honest and kind things than evil ones; than to say, the state of that ship is good to cross the Atlantic Ocean in, that is such as cannot hold together through the voyage, but will infallibly founder and sink by the way; under a notion that it may probably go great part of the way before it sinks, or that it will proceed and sail above water more hours than it will be in sinking: or to pronounce that road a good road to go to such a place, the greater part of which is plain and safe, though some parts of it are dangerous, and certainly fatal to them that travel in it; or to call that a good propensity, which is an inflexible inclination to travel in such a way.

A propensity to that sin which brings God's eternal wrath and curse (which has been proved to belong to the nature of man) is evil, not only as it is *calamitous* and *sorrowful*, ending in great *natural evil*, but as it is *odious* and *detestable*: for by the supposition, it tends to that *moral evil*, by which the subject becomes odious in the sight of God, and liable, as such, to be condemned, and utterly rejected, and cursed by him. This also makes it evident, that the state which it has been proved mankind are in, is a corrupt state in a *moral sense*, that it is inconsistent with the fulfilment of the law of God, which is the rule of moral rectitude and goodness. That tendency which is opposite to that which the moral law requires and insists upon, and prone to that which the moral law utterly forbids, and eternally condemns the subject for, is doubtless a corrupt tendency, in a moral sense.

So that this depravity is both *odious*, and also *pernicious*, fatal and destructive, in the highest sense, as inevitably tending to that which implies man's eternal ruin; it shows that man, as he is by nature, is in a deplorable and undone state, in the highest sense. And this proves that men do not come into the world perfectly innocent in the sight of God, and without any just exposedness to his displeasure. For the being by nature in a lost and ruined state, in the highest sense, is not consistent with being by nature in a state of favor with God.

But if any should still insist on a notion of men's good deeds exceeding their bad ones, and that, seeing the good that is in men is more than countervails the evil, they cannot be properly denominated evil; all persons and things being most properly denominated from that which prevails, and has the ascendant in them, I would say further, that,

I presume it will be allowed, that if there is in man's nature a tendency to guilt and ill desert, in a vast overbalance to virtue and merit; or a propensity to that sin, the evil and demerit of which is so great, that the value and merit that is in him, or in all the virtuous acts that ever he performs, are as nothing to it; then truly the nature of man may be said to be corrupt and evil.

That this is the true case, may be demonstrated by what is evident of the infinite heinousness of sin against God, from the nature of things. The heinousness of this must rise in some proportion to the obligation we are under to regard the Divine Being; and that must be in some proportion to his worthiness of regard; which doubtless is infinitely beyond the worthiness of any of our fellow creatures. But the merit of our respect or obedience to God is not infinite. The merit of respect to any being does not increase, but is rather diminished, in proportion to the obligations we are under in strict justice to pay him that respect. There is no great merit in paying a debt we owe, and by the highest possible obligations in strict justice are obliged to pay, but there is great demerit in refusing to pay it. That on such accounts as these there is an infinite demerit in all sin against God, which must therefore immensely outweigh all the merit which can be supposed to be in our virtue, I think, is capable of full demonstration; and that the futility of the objections which some have made against the argument, might most plainly be demonstrated. But I shall omit a particular consideration of the evidence of this matter from the nature of things, as I study brevity, and lest any should cry out, *Metaphysics!* as the manner of some is, when any argument is handled against any tenet they are fond of, with a close and exact consideration of the nature of things. And this is not so necessary in the present case, inasmuch as the point asserted, namely, that he who commits any one sin, has guilt and ill desert, which is so great, that the value and merit of all the good which it is possible he should do in his whole life, is as nothing to it; I say this point is not only evident by *metaphysics,* but is plainly demonstrated by what has been shown to be *fact,* with respect to God's own constitutions and dispensations towards mankind; as particularly by this, that whatever acts of virtue and obedience a man performs, yet if he trespasses in one point, is guilty of any the least sin, he, according to the law of God, and so according to the exact truth of things, and the proper demerit

of sin, is exposed to be wholly cast out of favor with God, and subjected to his curse, to be utterly and eternally destroyed. This has been proved, and shown to be the doctrine which Dr. Taylor abundantly teaches. But how can it be agreeable to the nature of things, and exactly consonant to everlasting truth and righteousness, thus to deal with a creature for the least sinful act, though he should perform ever so many thousands of honest and virtuous acts, to countervail the evil of that sin? Or how can it be agreeable to the exact truth and real demerit of things, thus wholly to cast off the deficient creature, without any regard to the merit of all his good deeds, unless that be in truth the case, that the value and merit of all those good actions, bear no proportion to the heinousness of the least sin? If it were not so, one would think, that however the offending person might have some proper punishment, yet, seeing there is so much virtue to lay in the balance against the guilt, it would be agreeable to the nature of things, that he should find some favor, and not be altogether rejected, and made the subject of perfect and eternal destruction; and thus no account at all be made of all his virtue, so much as to procure him the least relief or hope. How can such a constitution *represent sin in its proper colors,* and *according to its true nature and desert* (as Dr. Taylor says it does), unless this be its true nature, that it is so bad, that even in the least instance it perfectly swallows up all the value of the sinner's supposed good deeds, let them be ever so many. So that this matter is not left to our metaphysics or philosophy; the great Lawgiver, and infallible Judge of the universe, has clearly decided it, in the revelation he has made of what is agreeable to exact truth, justice, and the nature of things, in his revealed law, or rule of righteousness.

* * *

The sum of our duty to God, required in his law, is *love to God;* taking love in a large sense, for the true regard of our hearts to God, implying esteem, honor, benevolence, gratitude, complacence, &c. This is not only very plain by the Scripture, but it is evident in itself. The sum of what the law of God requires, is doubtless obedience to that law: no law can require more than that it be obeyed. But it is manifest, that obedience to God is nothing, any otherwise than as a testimony of the respect of our hearts to God: without the heart, man's external acts are no more than the motions of the limbs of a wooden image, have no more of the nature of either sin or righteousness. It must therefore needs be so, that love to God, or the respect of the heart, must be the sum of the duty required towards God in his law.

It therefore appears from the premises, that whosoever withholds more of that love or respect of heart from God, which his law requires, than he affords, has more sin than righteousness. Not only he that has less divine love, than passions and affections which are opposite; but also he that does not love God half so much as he ought, or has reason to do, has justly more wrong than right imputed to him; according to the law of God, and the law of reason, he has more irregularity than rectitude, with regard to the law of love. The sinful disrespect or unrespectfulness of his heart to God, is greater than his respect to him.

But what considerate person is there, even among the more virtuous part of mankind, but what would be ashamed to say, and profess before God or men, that he loves God half so much as he ought to do; or that he exercises one half of that esteem, honor and gratitude towards God, which would be altogether becoming him; considering what God is, and what great manifestations he has made of his transcendent excellency and goodness, and what benefits he receives from him? And if few or none of the best of men can with reason and truth make even such a profession, how far from it must the generality of mankind be?

The chief and most fundamental of all the commands of the moral law, requires us *"to love the Lord our God with all our hearts, and with all our souls, with all our strength, and all our mind";* that is plainly, with all that is within us, or to the utmost capacity of our nature; all that belongs *to,* or is comprehended *within* the utmost extent or capacity of our heart and soul, and mind and strength, is required. God is in himself worthy of infinitely greater love, than any creature can exercise towards him: he is worthy of love equal to his perfections, which are infinite: God loves himself with no greater love than he is worthy of, when he loves himself infinitely; but we can give God no more than we have. Therefore, if we give him so much, if we love him to the utmost extent of the faculties of our nature, we are excused; but when what is proposed, is only that we should love him as much as our capacity will allow, this excuse of want of capacity ceases, and obligation takes hold of us; and we are doubtless obliged to love God to the utmost of what is possible for us, with such faculties, and such opportunities and advantages to know God, as we have. And it is evidently implied in this great commandment of the law, that our love to God should be so great, as to have the most absolute possession of all the soul, and the perfect government of all the principles and springs of action that are in our nature. . . .

If we consider the love of God, with respect to that one kind of exercise of it, namely, *gratitude,* how far indeed do the generality of mankind come short of the rule of right and reason in this! If we consider how various, innumerable, and vast the benefits are we receive from God, and how infinitely great and wonderful that grace of his is, which is revealed and offered to them that live under the gospel, in that eternal salvation which is procured by God's giving his only begotten Son to die for sinners; and also how unworthy we are all, deserving (as Dr. Taylor confesses) eternal perdition under God's wrath and curse; how great is the gratitude that would become us, who are the subjects of so many and great benefits, and have such grace towards poor, sinful, lost mankind set before us in so affecting a manner, as in the extreme sufferings of the Son of God, being carried through those pains by a love stronger than death, a love that conquered those mighty agonies, a love whose length, and breadth, and depth, and height, passes knowledge? But oh! What poor returns! How little the gratitude! How low, how cold and inconstant the affection in the best, compared with the obligation! And what then shall be said of the gratitude of the generality? Or rather, who can express the ingratitude? . . .

How far the generality of mankind are from their duty with respect to love to God, will further appear, if we consider that we are obliged not only to love him with a love of gratitude for benefits received; but true love to God primarily consists in a supreme regard to him for what he is in himself. The tendency of true virtue is to treat every thing as it is,

and according to its nature. And if we regard the Most High according to the infinite dignity and glory of his nature, we shall esteem and love him with all our heart and soul, and to the utmost of the capacity of our nature, on this account; and not primarily because he has promoted our interest. If God be infinitely excellent in himself, then he is infinitely lovely on that account, or in other words, infinitely worthy to be loved. And doubtless, if he be worthy to be loved for this, then he ought to be loved for this. And it is manifest there can be no true love to him, if he be not loved for what he is in himself. For if we love him not for his own sake, but for something else, then our love is not terminated on him, but on something else, as its ultimate object. That is no true value for infinite worth, which implies no value for that worthiness in itself considered, but only on the account of something foreign. Our esteem of God is fundamentally defective, if it be not primarily for the excellency of his nature, which is the foundation of all that is valuable in him in any respect. If we love not God because he is what he is, but only because he is profitable to us, in truth we love him not at all; if we seem to love him, our love is not to him, but to something else.

* * *

But if we consider how men generally conduct themselves in things on which their well being does infinitely more depend, how vast is the diversity! In these things how cold, lifeless and dilatory! With what difficulty are a few of multitudes excited to any tolerable degree of care and diligence, by the innumerable means used with men to make them wise for themselves! And when some vigilance and activity is excited, how apt is it to die away, like a mere force against a natural tendency! What need of a constant repetition of admonitions and counsels to keep the heart from falling asleep! How many objections are made! And how are difficulties magnified! And how soon is the mind discouraged! How many arguments, and often renewed, and variously and elaborately enforced, do men stand in need of, to convince them of things that are self-evident! As that things which are eternal, are infinitely more important than things temporal, and the like. And after all, how very few are convinced effectually, or in such a manner as to induce to a practical preference of eternal things! How senseless are men to the necessity of improving their time to provide for futurity, as to their spiritual interest, and their welfare in another world! Though it be an endless futurity, and though it be their own personal, infinitely important good, after they are dead, that is to be cared for, and not the good of their children, which they shall have no share in. Though men are so sensible of the uncertainty of their neighbors' lives, when any considerable part of their estates depends on the continuance of them; how stupidly senseless do they seem to be of the uncertainty of their own lives, when their preservation from immensely great, remediless, and endless misery, is risked by a present delay, through a dependence on future opportunity! What a dreadful venture will men carelessly and boldly run, and repeat and multiply, with regard to their eternal salvation, who are very careful to have every thing in a deed or bond firm, and without a flaw! How negligent are they of their special advantages and opportunities for their soul's good! How hardly awakened by the most evident and imminent dangers, threatening eternal destruction, yea, though put in mind of them, and much pains taken to point them forth, show them plainly, and fully to represent them, if possible to engage their attention to them! How are they like the horse, that boldly rushes into the battle! How hardly are men convinced by their own frequent and abundant experience, of the unsatisfactory nature of earthly things, and the instability of their own hearts in their good frames and intentions! And how hardly convinced by their own observation, and the experience of all past generations, of the uncertainty of life, and its enjoyments!

Francis Hutcheson: MORALITY MEANS SEEKING
THE GENERAL GOOD

Francis Hutcheson (1694–1746) brought on controversy in England because of his writings in ethics. He argued for an innate "moral sense" in man. By this he meant that men called it good to promote the happiness of others. Right action was whatever secured the general welfare

From Francis Hutcheson, *An Inquiry into the Original of our Ideas of Beauty and Virtue* (2nd ed., London: J. Darby, etc., 1726), pp. 121–122, 133–135, 140–142, 180–181.

*of mankind. Private self-love could be considered the source of human
action because each individual man is part of general mankind, but
Hutcheson more often stressed the notion of "benevolence," by which
a man acts without regard to personal consequences. In addition to
this idea of benevolence as the spring of moral good, Hutcheson perceived a close correlation between virtue and beauty. Universal truths
are beautiful and moral action possesses harmony and proportion.*

IT IS TRUE indeed, that the actions
we approve in others, are generally
imagined to tend to the natural good of
mankind, or of some parts of it. But
whence this secret chain between each
person and mankind? How is my interest
connected with the most distant parts of
it? And yet I must admire actions which
are beneficial to them, and love the
author. Whence this love, compassion,
indignation and hatred toward even
feigned characters, in the most distant
ages, and nations, according as they appear kind, faithful, compassionate, or of
the opposite dispositions, toward their
imaginary contemporaries? If there is no
moral sense, which makes rational actions appear beautiful, or deformed; if
all approbation be from the interest of
the approver,

What's Hecuba to us, or we to Hecuba?

Some refined explainers of self-love
may tell us, "That we hate, or love characters, according as we apprehend we
should have been supported, or injured
by them, had we lived in their days."
But how obvious is the answer, if we only
observe, that had we no sense of moral
good in humanity, mercy, faithfulness,
why should not self-love, and our sense
of natural good engage us always to the
victorious side, and make us admire and
love the successful tyrant, or traitor?
Why do not we love Sinon, or Pyrrhus,
in the *Aeneid?* For had we been Greeks,
these two would have been very advan-

tageous characters. Why are we affected
with the fortunes of Priamus, Polites,
Choroebus or Aeneas? It is plain we
have some secret sense which determines
our approbation without regard to self-
interest; otherwise we should always
favor the fortunate side without regard
to virtue, and suppose ourselves engaged
with that party.

* * *

If what is said makes it appear that
we have some other amiable idea of actions than that of advantageous to ourselves, we may conclude, "That this perception of moral good is not derived
from custom, education, example, or
study." These give us no new ideas: they
might make us see advantage to ourselves in actions whose usefulness did not
at first appear; or give us opinions of
some tendency of actions to our detri-
ment, by some nice deductions of reason,
or by a rash prejudice, when upon the
first view of the action we should have
observed no such thing: but they never
could have made us apprehend actions
as amiable or odious, without any consideration of our own advantage.

It remains then, "That as the author
of nature has determined us to receive,
by our external senses, pleasant or disagreeable ideas of objects, according as
they are useful or hurtful to our bodies;
and to receive from uniform objects the
pleasures of beauty and harmony, to excite us to the pursuit of knowledge, and

to reward us for it; or to be an argument to us of his goodness, as the uniformity itself proves his existence, whether we had a sense of beauty in uniformity or not: in the same manner he has given us a moral sense, to direct our actions, and to give us still nobler pleasures; so that while we are only intending the good of others, we undesignedly promote our own greatest private good."

We are not to imagine, that this moral sense, more than the other senses, supposes any innate ideas, knowledge, or practical proposition: we mean by it only a determination of our minds to receive amiable or disagreeable ideas of actions, when they occur to our observation, antecedent to any opinions of advantage or loss to redound to ourselves from them; even as we are pleased with a regular form, or an harmonious composition, without having any knowledge of mathematics, or seeing any advantage in that form, or composition, different from the immediate pleasure.

* * *

As to the love of benevolence, the very name excludes self-interest. We never call that man benevolent, who is in fact useful to others, but at the same time only intends his own interest, without any desire of, or delight in, the good of others. If there be any benevolence at all, it must be disinterested; for the most useful action imaginable, loses all appearance of benevolence, as soon as we discern that it only flowed from self-love or interest. Thus, never were any human actions more advantageous, than the inventions of fire, and iron; but if these were casual, or if the inventor only intended his own interest in them, there is nothing which can be called benevolent in them. Wherever then benevolence

is supposed, there it is imagined disinterested, and designed for the good of others.

But it must be here observed, that as all men have self-love, as well as benevolence, these two principles may jointly excite a man to the same action; and then they are to be considered as two forces impelling the same body to motion; sometimes they conspire, sometimes are indifferent to each other, and sometimes are in some degree opposite. Thus, if a man have such strong benevolence, as would have produced an action without any views of self-interest; that such a man has also in view private advantage, along with public good, as the effect of his action, does no way diminish the benevolence of the action. When he would not have produced so much public good, had it not been for prospect of self-interest, then the effect of self-love is to be deducted, and his benevolence is proportioned to the remainder of good, which pure benevolence would have produced. When a man's benevolence is hurtful to himself, then self-love is opposite to benevolence, and the benevolence is proportioned to the sum of the good produced, added to the resistance of self-love surmounted by it. In most cases it is impossible for men to know how far their fellows are influenced by the one or other of these principles; but yet the general truth is sufficiently certain, that this is the way in which the benevolence of actions is to be computed. Since then, no love to rational agents can proceed from self-interest, every action must be disinterested, as far as it flows from love to rational agents.

* * *

All benevolence, even toward a part, is amiable, when not inconsistent with the good of the whole: but this is a smaller degree of virtue, unless our beneficence be restrained by want of power, and not want of love to the whole. All strict attachments to a part, as in natural affection, or virtuous friendships; or when some parts are so eminently useful to the whole, that even universal benevolence would determine us with special care and affection to study their interests. Thus universal benevolence would incline us to a more strong concern for the interests of great and generous characters in a high station, or make us more earnestly study the interests of any generous society, whose whole constitution was contrived to promote universal good. Thus a good fancy in architecture, would lead a man, who was not able to bear the expense of a completely regular building, to choose such a degree of ornament as he could keep uniformly through the whole, and not move him to make a vain unfinished attempt in one part, of what he foresaw he could not succeed in as to the whole. And the most perfect rules of architecture condemn an excessive profusion of ornament on one part, above the proportion of the whole, unless that part be some eminent place of the edifice, such as the chief front, or public entrance; the adorning of which would beautify the whole more than an equal expense of ornament on any other part.

*   *   *

Jonathan Edwards: MORALITY DEPENDS UPON BENEVOLENCE TO GOD

Although it was not published until 1765, after his death, Edwards wrote The Nature of True Virtue *in 1755. The work is remarkable if only because it is Edwards' least controversial and most speculative work. This may have been a new direction in his thought after years of warfare against Arminians, anti-revivalists, and personal enemies at Northampton. Yet it is consistent with his earlier writings. Human corruption and selfishness are the result of self-love, with no interest in God. In sharp contrast, true virtue is defined as disinterested benevolence, especially to God because God is most worthy of it. Edwards acquired the idea of benevolence from Hutcheson and developed it further by making it a question of metaphysics as well as of morality. Hutcheson's belief in the analogy of beauty and virtue stimulated Edwards to expand thoughts he had long held on the unity of goodness, truth and beauty.* True Virtue *seems to be an uncompleted work; it makes highly suggestive assertions which are not fully developed. This is unlike Edwards and he may have desired to write more before submitting it for publication. There are signs that the work may have been a fragmentary sketch for a new and comprehensive philosophy which was cut short by Edwards' death two years after* True Virtue *was written.*

From Jonathan Edwards, *The Works of President Edwards,* vol. II, pp. 266–271, 276–281, 287–289.

TRUE VIRTUE must chiefly consist in love to God; the Being of Beings, infinitely the greatest and best of Beings. This appears, whether we consider the primary or secondary ground of virtuous love. It was observed, that the *first* objective ground of that love wherein true virtue consists, is Being, simply considered: and as a necessary consequence of this, that Being who has the most of Being, or the greatest share of universal existence, has proportionably the greatest share of virtuous benevolence, so far as such a Being is exhibited to the faculties of our minds, other things being equal. But God has infinitely the greatest share of existence, or is infinitely the greatest Being. So that all other Being, even that of all created things whatsoever, throughout the whole universe, is as nothing in comparison of the Divine Being.

And if we consider the *secondary* ground of love, viz., beauty, or moral excellency, the same thing will appear. For as God is infinitely the greatest Being, so he is allowed to be infinitely the most beautiful and excellent: and all the beauty to be found diffused throughout the whole creation, is but the reflection of the diffused beams of that Being who hath an infinite fulness of brightness and glory. God's beauty is infinitely more valuable than that of all other Beings, upon both those accounts mentioned, viz., the *degree* of his virtue, and the greatness of the Being possessed of this virtue. And God has sufficiently exhibited himself, in his Being, his infinite greatness and excellency: and has given us faculties, whereby we are capable of plainly discovering immense superiority to all other Beings, in these respects. Therefore he that has true virtue, consisting in benevolence to Being in general, and in that complacence in virtue, or moral beauty, and benevolence to virtuous Being, must necessarily have a supreme love to God, both of benevolence and complacence. And all true virtue must radically and essentially, and as it were summarily, consist in this. Because God is not only infinitely greater and more excellent than all other Being, but he is the head of the universal system of existence; the foundation and fountain of all Being and all Beauty; from whom all is perfectly derived, and on whom all is most absolutely and perfectly dependent; *of whom* and *through whom,* and *to whom* is all Being and all perfection; and whose Being and beauty is as it were the sum and comprehension of all existence and excellence: much more than the sun is the fountain and summary comprehension of all the light and brightness of the day. . . .

There seems to be an inconsistence in some writers on morality, in this respect, that they do not wholly exclude a regard to the *Deity* out of their schemes of morality, but yet mention it so slightly, that they leave me room and reason to suspect they esteem it a less important and a subordinate part of true morality; and insist on benevolence to the *created system* in such a manner as would naturally lead one to suppose, they look upon that as by far the most important and essential thing. But why should this be? If true virtue consists partly in a respect to God, then doubtless it consists chiefly in it. If true morality requires that we should have some regard, some benevolent affection to our Creator, as well as to his creatures, then doubtless it requires the first regard to be paid to him; and that he be every way the supreme object of our benevolence. If his being above our reach, and beyond all capacity of being profited by us, does not hinder but that nevertheless he is the proper object of our love, then it does not hinder that he should be loved according to his dignity, or according to the degree in which he has those things wherein worthiness of regard consists so far as we are capable of it. But this worthiness none will deny consists in these two things, *greatness* and moral *goodness*. And those that own a God, do not deny that he infinitely exceeds all other Beings in these. If the Deity is to be looked upon as within that system of Beings which properly terminates our benevolence, or belonging to that whole, certainly he is to be regarded as the *head* of the system, and the *chief* part of it; if it be proper to call him a *part,* who is infinitely more than all the rest, and in comparison of whom and without whom all the rest are nothing, either as to beauty or existence. And therefore certainly, unless we will be atheists, we must allow that true virtue does primarily and most essentially consist in a supreme love to God; and that where this is wanting there can be no true virtue.

But this being a matter of the highest importance, I shall say something further to make it plain, that love to God is most essential to true virtue; and that no benevolence whatsoever to other Beings can be of the nature of true virtue, without it.

And therefore let it be supposed, that some Beings, by natural instinct, or by some other means, have a determination of mind to union and benevolence to a *particular person,* or *private system,* which is but a small part of the universal system of Being: and that this disposition or determination of mind is independent on, or not subordinate to benevolence, to *Being in general.* Such a determination, disposition, or affection of mind is not of the nature of true virtue.

This is allowed by all with regard to *self-love;* in which, good will is confined

to one single person only. And there are the same reasons, why any other private affection or good will, though extending to a society of persons, independent of, and unsubordinate to, benevolence to the universality, should not be esteemed truly virtuous. For, notwithstanding it extends to a number of persons, which taken together are more than a single person, yet the whole falls infinitely short of the universality of existence; and if put in the scales with it, has no greater proportion to it than a single person.

However, it may not be amiss more particularly to consider the reasons why *private affections,* or good will limited to a particular circle of Beings, falling infinitely short of the whole existence, and not dependent upon it, nor subordinate to general benevolence, cannot be of the nature of true virtue.

1. Such a private affection, detached from general benevolence and independent on it, as the case may be, will be *against* general benevolence, or of a contrary tendency; and will set a person *against* general existence, and make him an enemy to it. — As it is with *selfishness,* or when a man is governed by a regard to his own private interest, independent of regard to the public good, such a temper exposes a man to act the part of an enemy to the public. As, in every case wherein his private interest seems to clash with the public; or in all those cases wherein such things are presented to his view, that suit his personal appetites or private inclinations, but are inconsistent with the good of the public. On which account a selfish, contracted, narrow spirit is generally abhorred, and is esteemed base and sordid. — But if a man's affection takes in half a dozen more, and his regards extend so far beyond his own single person as to take in his children and family; or if it reaches further still,

to a longer circle, but falls infinitely short of the universal system, and is exclusive of Being in general; his private affection exposes him to the same thing, viz., to pursue the interest of its particular object in *opposition* to general existence; which is certainly contrary to the tendency to true virtue; yea, directly contrary to the main and most essential thing in its nature, the thing on account of which chiefly its nature and tendency is good. For the chief and most essential good that is in virtue, is its favoring Being in general. Now certainly, if private affection to a limited system had in itself the essential nature of virtue, it would be impossible, that it should in any circumstance whatsoever have a tendency and inclination directly *contrary* to that wherein the essence of virtue chiefly consists.

2. Private affection, if not subordinate to general affection, is not only liable, as the case *may* be, to issue in enmity to Being in general, but has a *tendency* to it as the case certainly *is*, and must necessarily be. For he that is influenced by private affection, not subordinate to regard to Being in general, sets up its particular or limited object above Being in general; and this most naturally tends to enmity against the latter, which is by right the great supreme, ruling, and absolutely sovereign object of our regard. Even as the setting up another prince as supreme in any kingdom, distinct from the lawful sovereign, naturally tends to enmity against the lawful sovereign. Wherever it is sufficiently published, that the supreme, infinite, and all comprehending Being requires a supreme regard to himself; and insists upon it, that our respect to him should universally rule in our hearts, and every other affection be subordinate to it, and this under the pain of his displeasure (as we must

suppose it is in the world of intelligent creatures, if God maintains a moral kingdom in the world); then a consciousness of our having chosen and set up another prince to rule over us, and subjected our hearts to him, and continuing in such an act, must unavoidably excite enmity, and fix us in a stated opposition to the Supreme Being. This demonstrates, that affection to a private society or system, independent on general benevolence, cannot be of the nature of true virtue. For this would be absurd, that it has the nature and essence of true virtue, and yet at the same time has a *tendency opposite* to true virtue.

3. Not only would affection to a private system, unsubordinate to regard to Being in general, have a tendency to opposition to the supreme object of virtuous affection, as its effect and consequence, but would become *itself* an opposition to that object. Considered by itself in its nature, detached from its effects, it is an instance of great opposition to the rightful supreme object of our respect. For it exalts its private object above the other great and infinite object; and sets that up as supreme, in opposition to this. It puts down Being in general, which is infinitely superior in itself and infinitely more important, in an inferior place; yea, subjects the supreme general object to this private infinitely inferior object; which is to treat it with great contempt, and truly to act in opposition to it, and to act in opposition to the true order of things, and in opposition to that which is infinitely the supreme interest; making this supreme and infinitely important interest, as far as in us lies, to be subject to, and dependent on, an interest infinitely inferior. This is to act against it, and to act the part of an enemy to it. He that takes a subject, and exalts him above his prince, sets him

as supreme instead of the prince, and treats his prince wholly as a subject, therein acts the part of an enemy to his prince.

From these things, I think, it is manifest, that no affection limited to any private system, not dependent on, nor subordinate to Being in general, can be of the nature of true virtue; and this, whatever the private system be, let it be more or less extensive, consisting of a greater or smaller number of individuals, so long as it contains an infinitely little part of universal existence, and so bears no proportion to the great all comprehending system. — And consequently, that no affection whatsoever to any creature, or any system of created Beings, which is not dependent on, nor subordinate to a propensity or union of the heart to God, the supreme and infinite Being, can be of the nature of true virtue. . . .

Hence it appears, that those *schemes* of religion or moral philosophy, which, however well in some respects they may treat of benevolence to *mankind,* and other virtues depending on it, yet have not a supreme regard to God, and love to him, laid in the *foundation,* and all other virtues handled in a *connection* with this, and in a *subordination* to this, are not true schemes of philosophy, but are fundamentally and essentially defective. And whatever other benevolence or generosity towards mankind, and other virtues, or moral qualifications which go by that name, any are possessed of, that are not attended with a *love to God* which is altogether above them, and to which they are subordinate, and on which they are dependent, there is nothing of the nature of true virtue or religion in them. — And it may be asserted in general that nothing is of the nature of true virtue in which God is not the *first* and the *last;* or which, with regard to

their exercises in general, have not their first foundation and source in apprehensions of God's supreme dignity and glory, and in answerable esteem and love of him, and have not respect to God as the supreme end.

*   *   *

Many assert, that all love arises from self-love. In order to determine this point, it should be clearly ascertained what is meant by self-love.

Self-love, I think, is generally defined — a man's love of his own happiness. Which is short, and may be thought very plain: but indeed is an ambiguous definition, as the pronoun *his own,* is equivocal, and liable to be taken in two very different senses. For man's *own happiness* may either be taken universally, for all the happiness and pleasure which the mind is in any regard the subject of, or whatever is grateful and pleasing to men; or it may be taken for the pleasure a man takes in his own proper, private, and separate good. — And so, *self-love* may be taken two ways.

1. Self-love may be taken for the same as his loving whatsoever is grateful or pleasing to him. Which comes only to this, that self-love is a man's liking, and being suited and pleased in that which he likes, and which pleases him; or, that it is a man's loving what he loves. For whatever a man loves, that thing is grateful and pleasing to him, whether that be his own peculiar happiness, or the happiness of others. And if this be all that they mean by self-love, no wonder they suppose that all love may be resolved into self-love. For it is undoubtedly true, that whatever a man loves, his love may be resolved into his loving what he loves — if that be proper speaking. If by self-love is meant nothing else but a man's

loving what is grateful or pleasing to him, and being averse to what is disagreeable, this is calling *that* self-love, which is only a general capacity of loving, or hating; or a capacity of being either pleased or displeased; which is the same thing as a man's having a faculty of will. For if nothing could be either pleasing or displeasing, agreeable or disagreeable to a man, then he could incline to nothing, and will nothing. But if he is capable of having inclination, will and choice, then what he inclines to, and chooses, is grateful to him; whatever that be, whether it be his own private good, the good of his neighbors, or the glory of God. And so far as it is grateful or pleasing to him, so far it is a part of his pleasure, good, or happiness.

But if this be what is meant by self-love, there is an impropriety and absurdity even in the putting of the question, Whether all our love, or our love to each particular object of our love, does not arise from self-love? For that would be the same as to inquire, Whether the reason why our love is fixed on such and such particular objects, is not, that we have a capacity of loving some things? This may be a general reason why men love or hate any thing at all; and therein differ from stones and trees, which love nothing, and hate nothing. But it can never be a reason why men's love is placed on such and such objects. That a man, in general, loves and is pleased with happiness, or (which is the same thing) has a capacity of enjoying happiness, cannot be the reason why such and such things become his happiness: as for instance, why the good of his neighbor, or the happiness and glory of God, is grateful and pleasing to him, and so becomes a part of his happiness.

Or if what they mean, who say that all love comes from self-love, be not, that

our loving such and such particular persons and things, arises from our love to happiness in general, but from a love to love our own happiness, which consists in these objects; so the reason why we love benevolence to our friends, or neighbors, is, because we love our happiness, consisting in their happiness, which we take pleasure in; — still the notion is absurd. For here the effect is made the cause of that, of which it is the effect: our happiness, consisting in the happiness of the person beloved, is made the cause of our love to that person. Whereas, the truth plainly is, that our love to the person is the cause of our delighting, or being happy in his happiness. How comes our happiness to consist in the happiness of such as we love, but by our hearts being first united to them in affection, so that we, as it were, look on them as ourselves, and so on their happiness as our own?

Men who have benevolence to others, have pleasure when they see others' happiness, because seeing their happiness gratifies some inclination that was in their hearts before. — They before inclined to their happiness; which was by benevolence or good will; and therefore when they see their happiness, their inclination is suited, and they are pleased. But the Being of inclinations and appetites is prior to any pleasure in gratifying these appetites.

2. Self-love, as the phrase is used in common speech, most commonly signifies a man's regard to his confined *private self*, or love to himself with respect to his *private interest*.

By *private* interest I mean that which most immediately consists in those pleasures, or pains, that are *personal*. For there is a comfort, and a grief, that some have in others' pleasures or pains; which are in others originally, but are derived to them, or in some measure become theirs, by virtue of a benevolent union of heart with others. And there are other pleasures and pains that are originally our own, and not what we have by such a participation with others. Which consist in preceptions agreeable, or contrary, to certain personal inclinations implanted in our nature; such as the sensitive appetites and aversions. Such also is the disposition or the determination of the mind to be pleased with external beauty, and with all inferior secondary beauty, consisting in uniformity, proportion, &c., whether in things external or internal, and to dislike the contrary deformity. Such also is the natural disposition in men to be pleased in a perception of their being the objects of the honor and love of others, and displeased with others' hatred and contempt. For pleasures and uneasinesses of this kind are doubtless as much owing to an immediate determination of the mind by a fixed law of our nature, as any of the pleasures or pains of external sense. And these pleasures are properly of the private and personal kind; being not by any participation of the happiness or sorrow of others, through benevolence. It is evidently mere self-love, that appears in this disposition. It is easy to see, that a man's love to himself will make him love love to himself, and hate hatred to himself. And as God has constituted our nature, self-love is exercised in no one disposition more than in this. Men, probably, are capable of much more pleasure and pain through this determination of the mind, than by any other personal inclination, or aversion, whatsoever. Though perhaps we do not so very often see instances of extreme suffering by this means, as by some others, yet we often see evidences of men's dreading the contempt of others more than death; and by such instances many conceive something

what men would suffer, if universally hated and despised; and many reasonably infer something of the greatness of the misery, that would arise under a sense of universal abhorrence, in a great view of intelligent Being in general, or in a clear view of the Deity, as incomprehensibly and immensely great, so that all other Beings are as nothing and vanity — together with a sense of his immediate continual presence, and an infinite concern with him and dependence upon him — and living constantly in the midst of most clear and strong evidences and manifestations of his hatred and contempt and wrath.

But to return. — These things may be sufficient to explain what I mean by private interest; in regard to which, self-love, most properly so called, is immediately exercised.

And here I would observe, that if we take self-love in this sense, so love to some others may truly be the effect of self-love; i. e., according to the common method and order, which is maintained in the laws of nature. For no created thing has power to produce an effect any otherwise than by virtue of the laws of nature. Thus that a man should love those that are of his party, when there are different parties contending one with another; and that are warmly engaged on his side, and promote his interest — this is the natural consequence of a private self-love. Indeed there is no metaphysical necessity, in the nature of things, that because a man loves himself, and regards his own interest, he therefore should love those that love him, and promote his interest; i. e., to suppose it to be otherwise, implies no contradiction. It will not follow from any absolute metaphysical necessity, that because bodies have solidity, cohesion, and gravitation towards the centre of the earth, therefore a weight suspended on the beam of a balance should have greater power to counterbalance a weight on the other side, when at a distance from the fulcrum, than when it is near. It implies no contradiction, that it should be otherwise: but only as it contradicts that beautiful proportion and harmony, which the author of nature observes in the laws of nature he has established. Neither is there any absolute necessity, the contrary implying a contradiction, that because there is an internal mutual attraction of the parts of the earth, or any other sphere, whereby the whole becomes one solid coherent body, therefore other bodies that are around it, should also be attracted by it, and those that are nearest, be attracted most. But according to the order and proportion generally observed in the laws of nature, one of these effects is connected with the other, so that it is justly looked upon as the same power of attraction in the globe of the earth, which draws bodies about the earth towards its centre, with that which attracts the parts of the earth themselves one to another; only exerted under different circumstances. By a like order of nature, a man's love to those that love him, is no more than a certain expression or effect of self-love. No other principle is needful in order to the effect, if nothing intervenes to countervail the natural tendency of self-love. Therefore there is no more true virtue in a man's thus loving his friends merely from self-love, than there is in self-love itself, the principle from whence it proceeds. So, a man's being disposed to hate those that hate him, or to resent injuries done him, arises from self-love in like manner as the loving those that love us, and being thankful for kindness shown us.

But it is said by some, that it is apparent, there is some other principle concerned in exciting the passions of gratitude and anger, besides self-love, viz., a moral sense, or sense of moral beauty and deformity, determining the minds of all mankind to approve of, and be pleased with virtue, and to disapprove of vice, and behold it with displicence; and that their seeing or supposing this moral beauty or deformity, in the kindness of a benefactor, or opposition of an adversary, is the occasion of these affections of gratitude or anger. Otherwise, why are not these affections excited in us towards inanimate things, that do us good, or hurt? Why do we not experience gratitude to a garden, or fruitful field? And why are we not angry with a tempest, or blasting mildew, or an overflowing stream? We are very differently affected towards those that do us good from the virtue of generosity, or hurt us from the vice of envy and malice, than towards things that hurt or help us, which are destitute of reason and will.

*   *   *

Natural conscience consists in these two things:

1. In that which has now been spoken of: that disposition to approve or disapprove the moral treatment which passes between us and others, from a determination of the mind to be easy, or uneasy, in a consciousness of our being consistent, or inconsistent with ourselves. Hereby we have a disposition to approve our own treatment of another, when we are conscious to ourselves that we treat him so as we should expect to be treated by him, were he in our case and we in his; and to disapprove of our own treatment of another, when we are conscious that we should be displeased, with the like treatment from him, if we were in his case. So we in our consciences approve of another's treatment of us, if we are conscious to ourselves, that if we were in his case, and he in ours, we

should think it just to treat him as he treats us; and disapprove his treatment of us, when we are conscious that we should think it unjust, if we were in his case. Thus men's consciences approve or disapprove the sentence of their judge, by which they are acquitted or condemned. — But this is not all that is in natural conscience. Besides this approving or disapproving from uneasiness as being inconsistent with ourselves, there is another thing that must precede it, and be the foundation of it. As for instance, when my conscience disapproves my own treatment of another, being conscious to myself that were I in his case, I should be displeased and angry with him for so treating me, the question might be asked, But what would be the ground of that supposed disapprobation, displeasure and anger, which I am conscious would be in me in that case? — That disapprobation must be on some other grounds. Therefore,

2. The other thing which belongs to the approbation or disapprobation of natural conscience, is the sense of desert, which was spoken of before; consisting, as was observed, in a natural agreement, proportion and harmony between malevolence or injury, and resentment and punishment; or between loving and being loved, between showing kindness and being rewarded, &c. Both these kinds of approving or disapproving concur in the approbation or disapprobation of conscience; the one founded on the other. Thus, when a man's conscience disapproves of his treatment of his neighbor, in the first place he is conscious that if he were in his neighbor's stead, he should resent such treatment, from a sense of justice, or from a sense of uniformity and equality between such treatment and resentment and punishment, as before explained. And then in the next

place he perceives, that therefore he is not consistent with himself, in doing what he himself should resent in that case; and hence disapproves it, as being naturally averse to opposition to himself.

Approbation and disapprobation of conscience, in the sense now explained, will extend to all virtue and vice; to every thing whatsoever that is morally good or evil, in a mind which does not confine its view to a private sphere, but will take things in general into its consideration, and is free from speculative error. For, as all virtue or moral good may be resolved into love to others, either God or creatures, so men easily see the uniformity and natural agreement there is between loving others, and being accepted and favored by others. And all vice, sin, or moral evil, summarily consisting in the want of this love to others, or in the contrary, viz., hatred or malevolence, so men easily see the natural agreement there is between hating and doing ill to others, and being hated by them and suffering ill by them, or from him that acts for all and has the care of the whole system. And as this sense of equality and natural agreement extends to all moral good and evil, so this lays a foundation of an equal extent with the other kind of approbation and disapprobation, which is grounded upon it, arising from an aversion to self-inconsistence and opposition. For in all cases of benevolence or the contrary towards others, we are capable of putting ourselves in the place of others, and are naturally led to do it, and so of reflecting, or being conscious to ourselves, how we should like or dislike such treatment from others. Thus natural conscience, if the understanding be properly enlightened, and errors and blinding stupifying prejudices are removed, concurs with the law of God, and is of equal extent with it, and joins its voice with it in every article.

And thus, in particular, we may see in what respect this natural conscience that has been described, extends to true virtue, consisting in union of heart to Being in general, and supreme love to God. For, although it sees not, or rather does not taste its primary and essential beauty, i. e., it tastes no sweetness in benevolence to Being in general, simply considered, or loves it not for Being in general's sake (for nothing but general benevolence itself can do that), yet this natural conscience, common to mankind, may approve of it from that uniformity, equality and justice, which there is in it, and the demerit which is seen in the contrary, consisting in the natural agreement between the contrary and being hated of Being in general. Men by natural conscience may see the justice (or natural agreement) there is in yielding all to God, as we receive all from God; and the justice there is in being his that has made us, and being willingly so, which is the same as being dependent on his will, and conformed to his will in the manner of our Being, as we are for our Being itself, and in the conformity of our will to his will, on whose will we are universally and most perfectly dependent; and also the justice there is in our supreme love to God, from his goodness — the natural agreement there is between our having supreme respect to him who exercises infinite goodness to us, and from whom we receive all well being. — Besides that disagreement and discord appears worse to natural sense (as was observed before) in things nearly related and of great importance; and therefore it must appear very ill, as it respects the infinite Being, and in that infinitely great relation which there is between the Creator and his creatures. And it is easy to conceive how that sense which is in natural conscience, should see the desert of punishment, which there is in the contrary of true virtue, viz., opposition and enmity to Being in general. For, this is only to see the natural agreement there is between opposing Being in general, and being opposed by Being in general; with a consciousness how that if we were infinitely great, we should expect to be regarded according to our greatness, and should proportionably resent contempt. Thus natural conscience, if well informed, will approve of true virtue, and will disapprove and condemn the want of it, and opposition to it; and yet without seeing the true beauty of it. Yea, if men's consciences were fully enlightened, if they were delivered from being confined to a private sphere, and brought to view and consider things in general, and delivered from being stupified by sensual objects and appetites, as they will be at the day of judgment, they would approve nothing but true virtue, nothing but general benevolence, and those affections and actions that are consistent with it, and subordinate to it. For they must see that consent to Being in general, and supreme respect to the Being of Beings, is most just; and that every thing which is inconsistent with it, and interferes with it, or flows from the want of it, is unjust, and deserves the opposition of universal existence.

Thus has God established and ordered, that this principle of natural conscience, which, though it implies no such thing as actual benevolence to Being in general, nor any delight in such a principle, simply considered, and so implies no truly spiritual sense or virtuous taste, yet should approve and condemn the same things that are approved and condemned by a spiritual sense or virtuous taste.

Jonathan Edwards: PHILOSOPHICAL DEFENSE OF REVIVALISM

Edwards had already written influential studies of revivalism by the time Religious Affections *was published in 1746. He was closely identified with the movement and was considered its leading apologist through three works:* A Faithful Narrative of the Surprising Work of God in the Conversion of Many Hundred Souls in Northampton *(1737),* The Distinguishing Marks of a Work of the Spirit of God *(1741), and* Some Thoughts Concerning the Present Revival of Religion in New England *(1743). This selection contains Edwards' primary explanation of religious experience in terms of the new Lockean psychology. Edwards went beyond Locke when he argued for a new "spiritual sense" and insisted that in the human mind, the will and affections are essentially the same. Edwards had the unique experience of using the latest Enlightenment thought to defend "enthusiasm" against the rationalists like Chauncy who still depended upon the older faculty psychology. Many scholars believe the* Religious Affections *was Edwards' most creative work. It was his final statement on the nature of revivalism.*

DOCTRINE. *True religion, in great part, consists in holy affections.* We see that the apostle, in observing and remarking the operations and exercises of religion in the Christians he wrote to, wherein their religion appeared to be true and of the right kind, when it had its greatest trial of what sort it was, being tried by persecution as gold is tried in the fire, and when their religion not only proved true, but was most pure, and cleansed from its dross and mixtures of that which was not true, and when religion appeared in them most in its genuine excellency and native beauty, and was found to praise, and honor, and glory; he singles out the religious affections of *love* and *joy,* that were then in exercise in them: these are the exercises of religion he takes notice of, wherein their religion did thus appear true and pure, and in its proper glory. Here I would,

1. Show what is intended by the affections.

2. Observe some things which make it evident, that a great part of true religion lies in the affections.

I. It may be inquired, what the affections of the mind are?

I answer: The affections are no other than the more vigorous and sensible exercises of the inclination and will of the soul.

God has endued the soul with two faculties: one is that by which it is capable of perception and speculation, or by which it discerns, and views, and judges of things; which is called the understanding. The other faculty is that by which the soul does not merely perceive and view things, but is some way inclined with respect to the things it views or considers; either is inclined *to* them, or is disinclined and averse *from* them; or is the faculty by which the soul does not behold things, as an indifferent unaffected spectator, but either as liking or disliking, pleased or displeased, approving or rejecting. This faculty is

From Edwards, *The Works of President Edwards,* vol. III, pp. 2–7, 71–72, 188, 195–196.

called by various names; it is sometimes called the *inclination:* and, as it has respect to the actions that are determined and governed by it, is called the *will:* and the mind, with regard to the exercises of this faculty, is often called the *heart.*

The exercise of this faculty are of two sorts; either those by which the soul is carried out towards the things that are in view, in approving of them, being pleased with them, and inclined to them; or those in which the soul opposes the things that are in view, in disapproving of them, and in being displeased with them, averse from them, and rejecting them.

And as the exercises of the inclination and will of the soul are various in their kinds, so they are much more various in their degrees. There are some exercises of pleasedness or displeasedness, inclination or disinclination, wherein the soul is carried but a little beyond a state of perfect indifference. — And there are other degrees above this, wherein the approbation or dislike, pleasedness or aversion, are stronger, wherein we may rise higher and higher, till the soul comes to act vigorously and sensibly, and the actings of the soul are with that strength, that (through the laws of the union which the Creator has fixed between the soul and the body) the motion of the blood and animal spirits begins to be sensibly altered; whence oftentimes arises some bodily sensation, especially about the heart and vitals, that are the fountain of the fluids of the body: from whence it comes to pass, that the mind, with regard to the exercises of this faculty, perhaps in all nations and ages, is called the *heart.* And, it is to be noted, that they are these more vigorous and sensible exercises of this faculty that are called the *affections.* The will, and the affections of the soul,

are not two faculties; the affections are not essentially distinct from the will, nor do they differ from the mere actings of the will, and inclination of the soul, but only in the liveliness and sensibleness of exercise.

It must be confessed, that language is here somewhat imperfect, and the meaning of words in a considerable measure loose and unfixed, and not precisely limited by custom, which governs the use of language. In some sense, the affection of the soul differs nothing at all from the will and inclination, and the will never is in any exercise any further than it is affected; it is not moved out of a state of perfect indifference, any otherwise than as it is affected one way or other, and acts nothing any further. But yet there are many actings of the will and inclination, that are not so commonly called *affections:* in every thing we do, wherein we act voluntarily, there is an exercise of the will and inclination; it is our inclination that governs us in our actions; but all the actings of the inclination and will, in all our common actions of life, are not ordinarily called affections. Yet, what are commonly called affections are not essentially different from them, but only in the degree and manner of exercise. In every act of the will whatsoever, the soul either likes or dislikes, is either inclined or disinclined to what is in view: these are not essentially different from those affections of love and hatred: that liking or inclination of the soul to a thing, if it be in a high degree, and be vigorous and lively, is the very same thing with the affection of love; and that disliking and disinclining, if in a greater degree, is the very same with hatred. In every act of the will for, or towards something not present, the soul is in some degree inclined to that thing; and that inclination, if in a considerable degree, is the very same with the affection of desire. And in every degree of the act of the will, wherein the soul approves of something present, there is a degree of pleasedness; and that pleasedness, if it be in a considerable degree, is the very same with the affections of joy or delight. And if the will disapproves of what is present, the soul is in some degree displeased, and if that displeasedness be great, it is the very same with the affection of grief or sorrow.

Such seems to be our nature, and such the laws of the union of soul and body, that there never is in any case whatsoever, any lively and vigorous exercise of the will or inclination of the soul, without some effect upon the body, in some alteration of the motion of its fluids, and especially of the animal spirits. And, on the other hand, from the same laws of the union of the soul and body, the constitution of the body, and the motion of its fluids, may promote the exercise of the affections. But yet it is not the body, but the mind only, that is the proper seat of the affections. The body of man is no more capable of being really the subject of love or hatred, joy or sorrow, fear or hope, than the body of a tree, or than the same body of man is capable of thinking and understanding. As it is the soul only that has ideas, so it is the soul only that is pleased or displeased with its ideas. As it is the soul only that thinks, so it is the soul only that loves or hates, rejoices or is grieved at what it thinks of. Nor are these motions of the animal spirits, and fluids of the body, any thing properly belonging to the nature of the affections, though they always accompany them, in the present state; but are only effects or concomitants of the affections that are entirely distinct from the affections themselves, and no way essential to them; so that an unbodied spirit

may be as capable of love and hatred, joy or sorrow, hope or fear, or other affections, as one that is united to a body.

The affections and passions are frequently spoken of as the same; and yet in the more common use of speech, there is in some respect a difference; and affection is a word that in its ordinary signification, seems to be something more extensive than passion, being used for all vigorous lively actings of the will or inclination; but passion for those that are more sudden, and whose effects on the animal spirits are more violent, and the mind more overpowered, and less in its own command.

As all the exercises of the inclination and will, are either in approving and liking, or disapproving and rejecting; so the affections are of two sorts; they are those by which the soul is carried out to what is in view, cleaving to it, or seeking it; or those by which it is averse from it, and opposes it.

Of the former sort are love, desire, hope, joy, gratitude, complacence. Of the latter kind are hatred, fear, anger, grief, and such like; which it is needless now to stand particularly to define. . . .

There are other mixed affections that might be also mentioned, but I hasten to,

II. The second thing proposed, which was to observe some things that render it evident, that true religion, in great part consists in the affections. And here,

1. What has been said of the nature of the affections makes this evident, and may be sufficient, without adding any thing further, to put this matter out of doubt; for who will deny that true religion consists in a great measure, in vigorous and lively actings of the inclination and will of the soul, or the fervent exercises of the heart?

That religion which God requires, and will accept, does not consist in weak, dull, and lifeless wishes, raising us but a little above a state of indifference: God, in his word, greatly insists upon it, that we be good in earnest, "fervent in spirit," and our hearts vigorously engaged in religion: Rom. xii. 11, "Be ye fervent in spirit, serving the Lord." Deut. x. 12, "And now, Israel, what doth the Lord thy God require of thee, but to fear the Lord thy God, to walk in all his ways, and to love him, and to serve the Lord thy God with all thy heart, and with all thy soul?" and chap. vi. 4, 6, "Hear, O Israel, the Lord our God is one Lord: And thou shalt love the Lord thy God with all thy heart, and with all thy might." It is such a fervent vigorous engagedness of the heart in religion, that is the fruit of a real circumcision of the heart, or true regeneration, and that has the promises of life; Deut. xxx. 6, "And the Lord thy God will circumcise thine heart, and the heart of thy seed, to love the Lord thy God with all thy heart, and with all thy soul, that thou mayest live."

If we be not in good earnest in religion, and our wills and inclinations be not strongly exercised, we are nothing. The things of religion are so great, that there can be no suitableness in the exercises of our hearts, to their nature and importance, unless they be lively and powerful. In nothing is vigor in the actings of our inclinations so requisite, as in religion; and in nothing is lukewarmness so odious. True religion is evermore a powerful thing; and the power of it appears, in the first place in the inward exercises of it in the heart, where is the principal and original seat of it. Hence true religion is called the *power of godliness*, in distinction from the external appearances of it, that are the *form* of it, 2 Tim. iii. 5: "Having a form of godliness, but denying the power of it." The Spirit of God, in those that have sound

and solid religion, is a spirit of powerful holy affection; and therefore, God is said "to have given the Spirit of power, and of love, and of a sound mind," 2 Tim. i. 7. And such, when they receive the Spirit of God, in his sanctifying and saving influences, are said to be "baptized with the Holy Ghost, and with fire;" by reason of the power and fervor of those exercises the Spirit of God excites in their hearts, whereby their hearts, when grace is in exercise, may be said to "burn within them;" as is said of the disciples, Luke xxiv. 32.

The business of religion is from time to time compared to those exercises, wherein men are wont to have their hearts and strength greatly exercised and engaged, such as running, wrestling or agonizing for a great prize or crown, and fighting with strong enemies that seek our lives, and warring as those, that by violence take a city or kingdom. . . .

2. The Author of the human nature has not only given affections to men, but has made them very much the spring of men's actions. As the affections do not only necessarily belong to the human nature, but are a very great part of it; so (inasmuch as by regeneration persons are renewed in the whole man, and sanctified throughout) holy affections do not only necessarily belong to true religion, but are a very great part of it. And as true religion is of a practical nature, and God hath so constituted the human nature, that the affections are very much the spring of men's actions, this also shows, that true religion must consist very much in the affections.

Such is man's nature, that he is very inactive, any otherwise than he is influenced by some affection, either love or hatred, desire, hope, fear, or some other. These affections we see to be the springs that set men agoing, in all the affairs of life, and engage them in all their pursuits: these are the things that put men forward, and carry them along, in all their worldly business; and especially are men excited and animated by these, in all affairs wherein they are earnestly engaged, and which they pursue with vigor. We see the world of mankind to be exceeding busy and active; and the affections of men are the springs of the motion: take away all love and hatred, all hope and fear, all anger, zeal, and affectionate desire, and the world would be, in a great measure motionless and dead; there would be no such thing as activity amongst mankind, or any earnest pursuit whatsoever. It is affection that engages the covetous man, and him that is greedy of worldly profits, in his pursuits; and it is by the affections, that the ambitious man is put forward in his pursuit of worldly glory; and it is the affections also that actuate the voluptuous man, in his pursuit of pleasure and sensual delights: the world continues, from age to age, in a continual commotion and agitation, in a pursuit of these things; but take away all affection, and the spring of all this motion would be gone, and the motion itself would cease. And as in worldly things, worldly affections are very much the spring of men's motion and action; so in religious matters, the spring of their actions is very much religious affection: he that has doctrinal knowledge and speculation only, without affection, never is engaged in the business of religion.

3. Nothing is more manifest in fact, than that the things of religion take hold of men's souls, no further than they affect them. There are multitudes that often hear the word of God, and therein hear of those things that are infinitely great and important, and that most nearly concern them, and all that is heard seems to be wholly ineffectual upon them, and to make no alteration in their disposition or behavior; and the reason is, they are not affected with what they hear. There are many that often hear of the glorious perfections of God, his almighty power and boundless wisdom, his infinite majesty, and that holiness of God, by which he is of purer eyes than to behold evil, and cannot look on iniquity, and the heavens are not pure in his sight, and of God's infinite goodness and mercy, and hear of the great works of God's wisdom, power and goodness, wherein there appear the admirable manifestations of these perfections; they hear particularly of the unspeakable love of God and Christ, and of the great things that Christ has done and suffered, and of the great things of another world, of eternal misery in bearing the fierceness and wrath of Almighty God, and of endless blessedness and glory in the presence of God, and the enjoyment of his dear love; they also hear the peremptory commands of God, and his gracious counsels and warnings, and the sweet invitations of the gospel; I say, they often hear these things and yet remain as they were before, with no sensible alteration in them, either in heart or practice, because they are not affected with what they hear; and ever will be so till they are affected. — I am bold to assert, that there never was any considerable change wrought in the mind or conversation of any person, by any thing of a religious nature, that ever he read, heard or saw, that had not his affections moved. Never was a natural man engaged earnestly to seek his salvation; never were any such brought to cry after wisdom, and lift up their voice for understanding, and to wrestle with God in prayer for mercy; and never was one humbled, and brought to the foot of God, from any thing that ever he heard or imagined of his own unworthiness and

deserving of God's displeasure; nor was ever one induced to fly for refuge unto Christ, while his heart remained unaffected. Nor was there ever a saint awakened out of a cold, lifeless frame, or recovered from a declining state in religion, and brought back from a lamentable departure from God, without having his heart affected. And in a word, there never was any thing considerable brought to pass in the heart or life of any man living, by the things of religion, that had not his heart deeply affected by those things.

* * *

. . . in those gracious exercises and affections which are wrought in the minds of the saints, through the saving influences of the Spirit of God, there is a new inward perception or sensation of their minds, entirely different in its nature and kind, from any thing that ever their minds were the subjects of before they were sanctified. For doubtless if God by his mighty power produces something that is new, not only in degree and circumstances, but in its whole nature, and that which could be produced by no exalting, varying, or compounding of what was there before, or by adding any thing of the like kind; I say, if God produces something thus new in a mind, that is a perceiving, thinking, conscious thing; then doubtless something entirely new is felt, or perceived, or thought; or, which is the same thing, there is some new sensation or perception of the mind, which is entirely of a new sort, and which could be produced by no exalting, varying, or compounding of that kind of perceptions or sensations which the mind had before; or there is what some metaphysicians call a new simple idea. If grace be, in the sense above described,

an entirely new kind of principle, then the exercises of it are also entirely a new kind of exercises. And if there be in the soul a new sort of exercises which it is conscious of, which the soul knew nothing of before, and which no improvement, composition, or management of what it was before conscious or sensible of, could produce, or any thing like it; then it follows that the mind has an entirely new kind of perception or sensation; and here is, as it were, a new spiritual sense that the mind has, or a principle of a new kind of perception or spiritual sensation, which is in its whole nature different from any former kinds of sensation of the mind, as tasting is diverse from any of the other senses; and something is perceived by a true saint, in the exercise of this new sense of mind, in spiritual and divine things, as entirely diverse from any thing that is perceived in them, by natural men, as the sweet taste of honey is diverse from the ideas men have of honey by only looking on it, and feeling of it. So that the spiritual perceptions which a sanctified and spiritual person has, are not only diverse from all that natural men have after the manner that the ideas or perceptions of the same sense may differ one from another, but rather as the ideas and sensations of different senses do differ. Hence the work of the Spirit of God in regeneration is often in Scripture compared to the giving a new sense, giving eyes to see, and ears to hear, unstopping the ears of the deaf, and opening the eyes of them that were born blind, and turning from darkness unto light. And because this spiritual sense is immensely the most noble and excellent, and that without which all other principles of perception, and all our faculties are useless and vain; therefore the giving this new sense, with the blessed fruits and effects of it in the soul, is compared to a raising the dead, and to a new creation.

This new spiritual sense, and the new dispositions that attend it, are no new faculties, but are new principles of nature. I use the word principles for want of a word of a more determinate signification. By a principle of nature in this place, I mean that foundation which is laid in nature, either old or new, for any particular manner or kind of exercise of the faculties of the soul; or a natural habit or foundation for action, giving a personal ability and disposition to exert the faculties in exercises of such a certain kind; so that to exert the faculties in that kind of exercises may be said to be his nature. So this new spiritual sense is not a new faculty of understanding, but it is a new foundation laid in the nature of the soul, for a new kind of exercises of the same faculty of understanding. So that new holy disposition of heart that attends this new sense is not a new faculty of will, but a foundation laid in the nature of the soul, for a new kind of exercises of the same faculty of will.

* * *

Again, the reason of this expression and effect of holy affections in the practice, appears from what has been observed of "a change of nature, accompanying such affections." Without a change of nature, men's practice will not be thoroughly changed. Until the tree be made good, the fruit will not be good. Men do not gather grapes of thorns, nor figs of thistles. The swine may be washed, and appear clean for a little while, but yet, without a change of nature he will still wallow in the mire. Nature is a more powerful principle of action, than any thing that opposes it: though it may be violently restrained for

a while, it will finally overcome that which restrains it: it is like the stream of a river, it may be stopped a while with a dam, but if nothing be done to dry the fountain, it will not be stopped always; it will have a course, either in its old channel, or a new one. Nature is a thing more constant and permanent, than any of those things that are the foundation of carnal men's reformation and righteousness. When a natural man denies his lust, and lives a strict, religious life, and seems humble, painful, and earnest in religion, it is not natural; it is all a force against nature; as when a stone is violently thrown upwards; but that force will be gradually spent; yet nature will remain in its full strength, and so prevails again, and the stone returns downwards. As long as corrupt nature is not mortified, but the principle left whole in a man, it is a vain thing to expect that it should not govern. But if the old nature be indeed mortified, and a new and heavenly nature infused, then may it well be expected, that men will walk in newness of life, and continue to do so to the end of their days.

* * *

And as the Scripture plainly teaches, that practice is the best evidence of the sincerity of professing Christians; so reason teaches the same thing. Reason shows, that men's deeds are better and more faithful interpreters of their minds, than their words. The common sense of all mankind, through all ages and nations, teaches them to judge of men's hearts chiefly by their practice, in other matters; as, whether a man be a loyal subject, a true lover, a dutiful child, or a faithful servant. If a man profess a great deal of love and friendship to another, reason teaches all men, that such a profession is not so great an evidence of his being a real and hearty friend, as his appearing a friend in deeds; being faithful and constant to his friend in prosperity and adversity, ready to lay out himself, and deny himself, and suffer in his personal interest, to do him a kindness. A wise man will trust to such evidence of the sincerity of friendship, further than a thousand earnest professions and solemn declarations, and most affectionate expressions of friendship in words. And there is equal reason why practice should also be looked upon as the best evidence of friendship towards Christ. Reason says the same that Christ said, in John xiv. 21, "He that hath my commandments, and keepeth them, he it is that loveth me." Thus if we see a man, who in the course of his life seems to follow and imitate Christ, and greatly to exert and deny himself for the honor of Christ, and to promote his kingdom and interest in the world; reason teaches, that this is an evidence of love to Christ, more to be depended on, than if a man only says he has love to Christ, and tells of the inward experiences he has had of love to him, what strong love he felt, and how his heart was drawn out in love at such and such a time, when it may be there appears but little imitation of Christ in his behavior, and he seems backward to do any great matter for him, or to put himself out of his way for the promoting of his kingdom, but seems to be apt to excuse himself whenever he is called to deny himself for Christ. So if a man, in declaring his experiences, tells how he found his heart weaned from the world, and saw the vanity of it, so that all looked as nothing to him, at such and such times, and professes that he gives up all to God, and calls heaven and earth to witness to it; but yet in his practice is violent in pursuing the world, and

what he gets he keeps close, is exceeding loth to part with much of it to charitable and pious uses, it comes from him almost like his heart's blood. But there is another professing Christian, that says not a great deal, yet in his behavior appears ready at all times to forsake the world, whenever it stands in the way of his duty, and is free to part with it at any time to promote religion and the good of his fellow creatures. Reason teaches, that the latter gives far the most credible manifestation of a heart weaned from the world. And if a man appears to walk humbly before God and men, and to be of a conversation that savors of a broken heart, appearing patient and resigned to God under affliction, and meek in his behavior amongst men; this is a better evidence of humiliation, than if a person only tells how great a sense he had of his own unworthiness, how he was brought to lie in the dust, and was quite emptied of himself, and saw himself nothing and all over filthy and abominable, &c. &c., but yet acts as if he looked upon himself one of the first and best of saints, and by just right the head of all the Christians in the town, and is assuming, self-willed, and impatient of the least contradiction or opposition; we may be assured in such a case, that a man's practice comes from a lower place in his heart than his profession. So (to mention no more instances) if a professor of Christianity manifests in his behavior a pitiful tender spirit towards others in calamity, ready to bear their burdens with them, willing to spend his substance for them, and to suffer many inconveniences in his worldly interest to promote the good of others' souls and bodies; is not this a more credible manifestation of a spirit of love to men, than only a man's telling what love he felt to others at certain times, how he pitied their souls, how his soul was in travail for them, and how he felt hearty love and pity to his enemies; when in his behavior he seems to be of a very selfish spirit, close and niggardly, all for himself, and none for his neighbors, and perhaps envious and contentious? Persons in a pang of affection may think they have a willingness of heart for great things, to do much and to suffer much, and so may profess it very earnestly and confidently, when really their hearts are far from it. Thus many in their affectionate pangs, have thought themselves willing to be damned eternally for the glory of God. Passing affections easily produce words; and words are cheap; and godliness is more easily feigned in words than in actions. Christian practice is a costly, laborious thing. The self-denial that is required of Christians, and the narrowness of the way that leads to life, does not consist in words, but in practice. Hypocrites may much more easily be brought to talk like saints, than to act like saints.

V. THE CONTINUING CONTROVERSY OVER THE SIGNIFICANCE OF EDWARDS

Vernon L. Parrington: JONATHAN EDWARDS WAS AN ANACHRONISM

Vernon L. Parrington (1871–1929) wrote his three-volume intellectual history, Main Currents in American Thought *(1927–1930), from a liberal and progressive point of view. He suggested that an American national spirit was formed out of the conflict between progress and reaction, in which the forces of reason, optimism, democracy and freedom of thought won their struggle against irrationalism, pessimism, aristocracy and religious dogmatism. According to Parrington, Jonathan Edwards' presence amidst the growing liberalism of the eighteenth century was that of an outdated anachronism, whose primary influence was to delay the emergence of modern America. Religion repressed human freedom and progress, while environmental and economic forces, like the frontier and capitalism, encouraged creative human intellectual development.*

NEVER HAD the traditional theology been so sorely in need of a champion as at the beginning of the second quarter of the eighteenth century; and such a champion God raised up — many devout Calvinists believed — in the person of Jonathan Edwards. Armed at all points — a theologian equipped with the keenest dialectics, a metaphysician endowed with a brilliantly speculative mind, a psychologist competent to deal with the subtlest phenomena of the sick soul — here was a man who might be counted on to justify the ancient dogmas to the troubled churches of New England. . . .

In his early years, before his conversion turned him aside from his true path, setting the apologetics of the theologian above the speculations of the philosopher, Edwards gave promise of becoming a strikingly creative thinker. Following the native bent of his genius, he plunged into the study of metaphysics with such fruitful results that it seemed likely that New England Puritanism was at last to come to flower; that the mystical perception of the divine love, which had steeped the early Puritan thought in emotion and quickened it to poetry, was now to create a system of philosophy which, like transcendentalism in the next century, should adequately express the aspirations of the New England mind. There is no more interesting phase in the early history of Edwards than the transition from religious mysticism to philosophical idealism. The yearning for the knitting of the soul to Christ, as expressed in the imagery of the Song of

From *Main Currents in American Thought: The Colonial Mind, 1620–1800* by Vernon L. Parrington, copyright, 1927, by Harcourt, Brace and World, Inc.; renewed, 1955, by Vernon L. Parrington, Jr., Louise P. Tucker, Elizabeth P. Thomas. Reprinted by permission of the publishers. Pp. 152–156, 158–159, 162–163.

Songs, burgeoned into a larger idealism that translated the Rose of Sharon and the Lily of the Valley into an all-pervasive spirit of divine life. In certain moods it is the mystic who cries, "My soul breaketh for the longing it hath; my soul waiteth for the Lord, more than they who watch for the morning."

He was reading one day the words of Scripture [says Allen, paraphrasing Edwards' diary], "Now unto the King eternal, immortal, invisible, the only wise God, be honor and glory forever, Amen," when there came to him for the first time a sort of inward, sweet delight in God and divine things. A sense of the divine glory was, as it were, diffused through him. He thought how happy he should be if he might be rapt up to God in Heaven, swallowed up in him forever. He began to have an inward, sweet sense of Christ and the work of redemption. The Book of Canticles attracted him as a fit expression for his mood. It seemed to him as if he were in a kind of vision, alone in the mountains or some solitary wilderness conversing sweetly with Christ and wrapt and swallowed up in God. . . . God's Excellency, his wisdom, his purity and love, seemed to appear in everything — in the sun, moon, and stars; in clouds and blue sky; in the grass, flowers, trees; in the water and all nature, which used greatly to fix my mind.

In other moods the intellect gains ascendency over the emotions, and it is the idealistic metaphysician who speaks. With a searching curiosity that impelled him to ask what lies behind the outward semblance of things, binding them into a coherent whole and imparting to the world of experience a compelling unity, he came early to an interpretation distinctly Berkeleyan. From what source he derived it has been much debated and remains unanswered; nevertheless it is clear that it is closely related to his religious mysticism. When he inquired what lies back of the outward semblance, what is the thing in itself behind attributes and qualities, the existence of which is implicit in our perception of time and space, but which cannot be resolved into the things perceived, it was natural that he should have interpreted this *Ding an sich* in terms of God. "Men are wont to content themselves by saying merely that it is something; but that something is *He* in whom all things consist." The world of sensation thus translates itself into a world of ideas; and this world of ideas, the expression of the divine mind, is the only reality. The more important of his early generalizations are given by Allen in some extracts from his notes on the "Mind": "Bodies have no existence of their own." "All existence is mental; the existence of all things is ideal." "The brain exists only mentally, or in idea." "Instead of matter being the only proper substance, and more substantial than anything else because it is hard and solid, yet it is truly nothing at all, strictly and in itself considered." "The universe exists nowhere but in the divine mind." "Space is necessary, eternal, infinite, and omnipresent. But I had as good speak plain. I have already said as much as that space is God." "And indeed the secret lies here, — that which truly is the substance of all bodies is the infinitely exact and precise and perfectly stable Idea in God's mind, together with His stable will that the same shall gradually be communicated to us, and to other minds, according to certain fixed and exact established methods and laws; or, in somewhat different language, the infinitely exact, precise, Divine Idea, together with the answerable, perfectly exact, precise, and stable will, with respect to correspondent communications to created minds and effects on their minds."

Edwards had come to such conclusions before the normal unfolding of his mind was interrupted by his conversion. From the first a strong bias toward theology had tended to warp his interest in the purely metaphysical, and with the quickening of an active religious experience, he turned to examine the dogmas which expressed his faith. The call of the churches in distress came to him, and he made ready his logic to do battle with the enemy. Against the twin tendencies that were undermining the foundations of Calvinism — Arminianism with its humanistic emphasis and deism with its mechanistic — the deepest instincts of Edwards protested. The profound God-consciousness that filled him was stirred by what seemed an infidel attack upon the divine glory and sufficiency; the mystic and idealist was aroused to protest against a theology that conceived of religion as consisting of benevolence toward men rather than in union with God; and against a philosophy that in constructing a mechanical system was depersonalizing God into a vague First Cause, and bowing him politely out of the universe. In so great a crisis his duty seemed clear — to vindicate, not the ways of God, but God himself to men; to assert the glory and sufficiency of God even to the extent of minifying the capacities and potentialities of man.

The basis of his defense was already provided in his metaphysics, the conception of the divine idea existent in God's mind and expressed in His stable will. The needs of his polemics, however, thrust into relief the secondary rather than the primary element in his philosophy, exalting the doctrine of the divine will to the obscuring of the divine idea. How this came about is sufficiently clear in the light of the fact that in explaining the existence of evil, Calvinism fell back

on determinism: the dogma of election could be fitted to the conception of a precise and stable will of God. The long feud between Arminianism and Calvinism resulted from emphasis laid upon different attributes of the Godhood. Shall God be interpreted in terms of will or love? If He is the sovereign ruler of the universe, He is also the common father; and that which broadly divides later theological systems from earlier is the shift from the former interpretation to the latter. The strategic weakness of Edwards's position lay in his assumption of the divine sovereignty as a cardinal postulate.

But in adhering to the doctrine of predetermined election by the sovereign will of God, Edwards did unconscious violence to the instincts of the mystic, that throughout his earlier speculations — and in much of his later, as well — impelled him to glorify the love of God the Father, and the sweetness of spiritual communion with Him. The practical necessities of the preacher, called upon to uphold the dogma of election in face of growing disbelief, seem to have forced him to such a position; but once having entered upon the train of speculation opened by the question of divine polity involved in "His having mercy on whom He will have mercy, while whom He will, He hardeneth," he came somewhat reluctantly to accept the doctrine of God's sovereignty as the cardinal principle of his theology, the creative source of his thinking. Thereafter he followed a path that led back to an absolutist past, rather than forward to a more liberal future. He had broken wholly with the social tendencies of his age and world.

* * *

He was at the dividing of the ways;

he must abandon transcendentalism or the dogma of total depravity.

Instead he sought refuge in compromise, endeavoring to reconcile what was incompatible. Herein lay the tragedy of Edwards's intellectual life; the theologian triumphed over the philosopher, circumscribing his powers to ignoble ends. The field of efficiency allotted by the later theologian to this "in-dwelling vital principle," was no longer coextensive with the universe, but was narrowed to the little world of the elect. In the primal state of man, Edwards argued, before the sin of Adam had destroyed the harmony between creature and creator, the light which flowed from God as from a sun shone freely upon His universe, filling its remotest parts with the divine plenitude; but with the fall the harmony was destroyed, the sun was hidden, and only stray beams broke through the rifts to shine upon those whom God willed them to shine upon; all else in creation was given over to eternal darkness. And if the natural man, thus cast into sudden darkness "as light ceases in a room when the candle is withdrawn," is a being whose will is impotent to his salvation, it follows that he will now be impelled as inevitably towards evil as before he was impelled towards good. Every instinct of a nature corrupt and compact of sin, and with no wish to exchange darkness for light — having no eyes for the divine glory — drives him to a blind and consuming hatred of God. He is become as a loathsome "viper, hissing and spitting poison at God," the outcast and pariah of the universe. There is no drawing back from the conclusion involved in the argument; the Edwardean logic moves forward by regular steps. The punishment meted out to sin is to be measured by the excellence of which the sin is a denial. God is of infinite excellence, and denial of His excellence is therefore infinitely sinful and merits infinite punishment. As a perfectly just judge God could not decree otherwise; because of the infinite heinousness of his sin, the natural man must receive the doom of eternal damnation.

Under the rod of such logic — grotesque, abortive, unseasoned by any saving knowledge of human nature — Edwards preached that remarkable series of imprecatory sermons that sank deep into the memory of New England, and for which it has never forgiven him. Unfortunate as those sermons were in darkening the fame of an acute thinker, disastrous as they were in providing a sanction for other men to terrify the imaginations of ill-balanced persons, we cannot regret that Edwards devoted his logic to an assiduous stoking of the fires of hell. The theology of Calvin lay like a heavy weight upon the soul of New England, and there could be no surer way to bring it into disrepute, than to thrust into naked relief the brutal grotesqueries of those dogmas that professed thus to explain the dark mysteries which lie upon the horizons of life. For a long while yet they were to harass the imagination of New England, but the end already could be foreseen. Once the horrors that lay in the background of Calvinism were disclosed to common view, the system was doomed.

*   *   *

As one follows the laborious career of this great thinker, a sense of the tragic failure of his life deepens. The burdens that he assumed were beyond the strength of any man. Beginning as a mystic, brooding on the all-pervasive spirit of sweetness and light diffused through the universe, with its promise of spiritual emancipation; then turning to an archaic theology and giving over his middle years to the work of minifying the excellence of man in order to exalt the sovereignty of God; and finally settling back upon the mystical doctrine of conversion — such a life leaves one with a feeling of futility, a sense of great powers baffled and wasted, a spiritual tragedy enacted within the narrow walls of a minister's study. There was both pathos and irony in the fate of Jonathan Edwards, removed from the familiar places where for twenty years he had labored, the tie with his congregation broken, and sent to the frontier mission at Stockbridge to preach to a band of Indians and to speculate on the unfreedom of the human will. The greatest mind of New England had become an anachronism in a world that bred Benjamin Franklin. If he had been an Anglican like Bishop

Berkeley, if he had mingled with the leaders of thought in London instead of remaining isolated in Massachusetts, he must have made a name for himself not unworthy to be matched with that of the great bishop whom he so much resembled. The intellectual powers were his, but the inspiration was lacking; like Cotton Mather before him, he was the unconscious victim of a decadent ideal and a petty environment. Cut off from fruitful intercourse with other thinkers, drawn away from the stimulating field of philosophy into the arid realm of theology, it was his fate to devote his noble gifts to the thankless task of re-imprisoning the mind of New England within a system from which his nature and his powers summoned him to unshackle it. He was called to be a transcendental emancipator, but he remained a Calvinist.

Ola E. Winslow: THE TRAGEDY OF JONATHAN EDWARDS

Ola Elizabeth Winslow won the Pulitzer Prize for her 1940 biography of Edwards. Her portrait follows neither the grim image provided by Parrington nor does it turn Edwards into the contemporary modern indicated by Perry Miller. Winslow admits that Edwards' life had traditional religion at its core, yet he enjoyed the intellectual delights of the new philosophy in the Age of Reason. She suggests that Edwards was a man clouded by mystery, with a mind torn between the old and new, and burdened with constant tumult. Finally, however, Edwards was victorious in a manner that knit together and even transcended the conflicting forces of the eighteenth century.

THE FIRST signal honor of his career outside of his own parish was a tribute to a sermon he had preached. This was in 1731, when he was twenty-seven years old and had been settled in Northampton for more than four years. He had been invited by the Boston clergy to preach at the Public Lecture on July

Reprinted by permission of The Macmillan Company from *Jonathan Edwards, 1703–1758* by Ola Elizabeth Winslow. © The Crowell-Collier Publishing Company, 1961. Pp. 145–150, 297–301.

8th, and his sermon had so greatly pleased the older brethren that they had urged him to print it at once. This was his first publication.

In the light of his career as a revival preacher, the sermon is of considerable importance, for it laid the foundation of his whole evangelical structure. He called it *God Glorified in Man's Dependence*. It is a carefully reasoned discourse in which he made bold to announce that he could justify the ways of God to men by the basic tenet of traditional Calvinism, divine sovereignty. One cannot of course assign single causes to the complicated process of social change; and yet, fitted into its chronological place, this sermon appears to mark the beginning of both the new emphasis in doctrine and the new fervor in preaching which ten years later were to bring about the Great Awakening.

In 1731, New England was full of very disturbing signs of interest in the more modern plan of salvation loosely called Arminianism. In place of the familiar doctrines of God's sovereignty, His inexorable justice in the damnation of sinners, and the complete helplessness of men to do anything about it all, this new way of thinking held out hope by way of more respectable living, benevolence, and those measurable virtues generally known as "good works." These newer notions had the great advantage of being more concrete, easier to understand, and far more comfortable than the traditional sound doctrines. The conservative clergy were alarmed in proportion as the laity were interested, but in their great concern to speak against the new they had forgotten to preach the old. Here was a young man who, without calling the offensive new doctrine by name, preached the old with such fervor as to make it appear the more desirable. The Boston

clergy were delighted, and no wonder.

In Jonathan Edwards' personal story, this sermon made clear what was to be his lifelong theological loyalty. As between the "ancients" and the "moderns," he declared for the "ancients." The "fashionable new divinity," as he saw it, robbed God of his due glory and thwarted the whole scheme of human redemption as God had designed it. In this sermon he was not concerned to argue against these newer doctrines, or even to chart the true scheme of salvation as a consistent whole. He said nothing about eternal punishment, contrition for sin, or even conversion but, logician that he was, went back to the beginnings. The sovereignty of God in the world he had created was the foundation of all right doctrine. Until man had acknowledged this sovereignty unequivocally and had admitted his own helplessness, the gift of free grace could have no meaning for him. Having reasserted this absolute supremacy, Jonathan Edwards went on to define it in terms of personal redemption:

Man is nothing; God is all.
Man's very desire for God is God-given.
Whatever degree of holiness man may attain is not his own, but God's dwelling in him.
God communicates his own beauty to the souls of his saints.

In doctrine, this is pure Calvinism, purer in fact than New England was accustomed to hearing. In emphasis, it was a timely rebuke to those who were taking credit to themselves for any good works they practiced. In approach, it was frankly speculative; there was hardly a concrete detail in the whole sermon.

Stripped of the young eloquence with which they were proclaimed, these ideas were thoroughly familiar to the Boston divines who listened so approvingly. No phrase had been on the lips of the New England clergy more frequently since Jonathan Edwards was born than "sovereignty of God"; and yet, as he now interpreted this venerable doctrine, he seemed to be preaching a fresh, new truth. The sermon, as the record reads, was "uncommonly impressive." It is easy to see why. Back of the familiar structure of Calvinistic thought, in this basic first *Point,* "sovereignty," the fervent young preacher was putting the authority of his own personal religious experience. When he spoke of a satisfying spiritual joy, "a kind of effusion of God in the soul," he was not speaking the language of catechetical divinity as he had learned it in Ames' *Medulla* during his Yale College days; he was speaking out of his own knowledge of spiritual things. Divine sovereignty, by this interpretation, was the doctrine which, hitherto "abhorrent," had immediately after his conversion appeared "exceeding pleasant, bright and sweet." It would be years yet before he would clarify to his own complete intellectual satisfaction the complex psychology implicit in this inner change which he now proclaimed; but throughout his life the communication of God's own beauty to his redeemed creatures, not by virtue of any worthiness in them but by his own sovereign pleasure alone, would be to him the essence of religion, as man might begin to know it on earth. This Boston sermon of 1731 supplies the doctrinal basis for this first step in Jonathan Edwards' own pilgrim's progress.

In the long history of New England preaching, this sermon is not more important as a check to the fashionable new doctrine of salvation than to the much older process of rationalization by which the unfathomable, unpredictable God of Calvin had been gradually changed into a reasonable being. In fact, Calvin's God had not crossed to the American continent at all, but by 1620 had already suffered comfortable modification at the hands of various Cambridge divines: John Preston, William Perkins, Richard Sibbes, and notably William Ames, whose *Medulla Sacrae Theologiae* became the *vade mecum* of Harvard and Yale divinity students for another hundred years. During this same first century, New England Dissent through its own spokesmen, John Cotton, Thomas Hooker, John Davenport, and Peter Bulkeley, had modified Calvinistic doctrine still further in the direction of a reasonable rather than an arbitrary God, until by 1731 a theological system with a strongly legalistic bias had been developed. The "covenant of grace" amounted in effect to a contract, almost as binding on God as on man. Salvation was on terms. God bestowed it. Man did not deserve it, but he might know the terms, and if he chose to fulfil them, God was virtually in his power. God would keep His word. As a reasonable Being, he had to, except perhaps in the hundredth instance. Rationality left a small unplotted area for the inexplicable freakishness of Providence; but, generally speaking, the arbitrariness of an inscrutable Deity had been brought within predictable bounds. Neither the sovereignty of God nor the depravity of man had been denied, but both had been decidedly breached.

Even the great and awesome doctrine of election had come to mean, in practical pulpit treatment, that the slightest desire after salvation might be God's way of announcing to individual man that he was elected. If he would act on this suggestion, repent, submit himself to God, he might possibly be admitted. God spoke through His ordinances, of which preaching was one. Hence, if a man would only go to church, put himself under sermons (and also the watchful eye of the minister, God's appointed agent), his chance of salvation was greater than if he had not been exposed. Solomon Stoddard had made it still easier by suggesting that the sacred seal of the Lord's Supper might also, under special conditions, be a "converting ordinance." From such arguments it had been only one more step, and a short one, to say that "good works" also might put one in the way of faith. Calvin would have been incapable of such notions. His scorn of them and their proponents would have been sublime. With all his inexorable partiality, or rather because of it, the God of Calvin's *Institutes* dilates the imagination, whereas, by comparison, the God of Ames' *Medulla* merely commands respect. A man might almost deal with such a Being if he knew the answers, and they were all in Ames' *Medulla.* To borrow Calvin's own words, used by him to excoriate those who had imagined God to be corporeal, "the immensity and spirituality of the essence of God" had been accommodated to the narrow capacity of those who could not grasp his true majesty.

Without meaning to be a better Calvinist than his brethren, or even faintly imagining that he was, Jonathan Edwards in this 1731 sermon was predicating a Deity more fit for adoration than for finite comprehension. God was once again inscrutable, immutable, unpredictable. Man's place was in the dust, and when he had once caught a glimpse of the divine glory, he would willingly be there. Later, with other preachers of the Great Awakening, he put the dynamic of fear behind this same doctrine, emphasizing the glory of God in man's damnation; but on this earlier occasion

he was content to dwell on the transcendent glory of a Being upon whom men were utterly dependent. In his young fervor for this cardinal doctrine of a lost golden age, the older men were heartened, for they did spy a kind of hope.

The intense conviction of the young preacher, the approbation of the older men, and the far-reaching consequences of this check to newer theological ideas suggest another occasion in American religious history, arresting in its correspondence and also in its direct antithesis. On another July day, a little more than a century later, another young man, similarly quiet-voiced and without gestures, leaned on one elbow and read from a closely written manuscript to another ministerial company, met in Cambridge, three miles away. His words also were uncommonly impressive as he proclaimed man's dependence on God and the satisfying joy of that inner certainty which he also had learned through a personal experience of religion:

If a man is at heart just, then in so far is he God; the safety of God, the immortality of God, the majesty of God do enter into that man with justice.

One man was true to what is in you and me. He saw that God incarnates himself in man and evermore goes forth anew to take possession of his World. . . .

When this later address was finished, no one urged publication or offered to write a flattering preface. The settled ministry went out in rage and consternation, feeling that the temple had been polluted and the cause dishonored. But the souls of the young men were "roused"; they thronged around the speaker as though they had heard a prophet. A generation had been liberated by his words.

What Emerson did was to reassert in quite untheological language the life principle of all religion. To him creeds and theological systems crushed it to death. On the authority of his own vision, he swept them all aside, and said: The Kingdom of God is within you. Forget the creeds and find God for yourself today and tomorrow. Those who identified religion with current theological explanations of it were horrified. What Jonathan Edwards had done a hundred years earlier was to take the life principle of all religion, as he had found it out by his own search, vital and joy-giving, and shut it up in the husk of a dead idiom. He translated a personal experience into a theological system, and a system of which forward-looking men, even among the clergy, had begun to be disrespectful. No wonder those zealous for the old system were heartened. They felt the glow behind the words of this new herald, and thought (wrongly) that the life was in the system he justified. Perhaps this new champion might yet save a dying cause.

The comparison is doubtless unfair. In the history of men's thought a century can be a long time, nor does one read the record backward. Before Emerson began to think for himself, three more generations of courage in thought and action had been built into his heritage. On many paths men had dared to clear away the underbrush of tradition and to look on the bare contours of truth according to life. Emerson was the product of a far mellower culture and had had a few glimpses of the world beyond his own door. Besides, he was a man of intuition, and something of a poet. He could take a leap into the unknown, with no logician's sense to retard his progress. It would have been asking a great deal in 1731, although the like has sometimes

happened in the history of thought, for Jonathan Edwards, hedged in as he was by sound doctrine and shackled by too great reverence for authority, to dare to look into his own heart and speak what he knew, independently of all learned divines, past and present. If instead of justifying "vital piety" by the doctrines of Calvinism, he could only have looked past Calvin, past Luther, and past St. Augustine, back to the Sermon on the Mount, putting religion of the spirit in language that the rank and file could understand, there is no telling how the religious history of America and the cultural pattern of America might have been altered. He had the courage. He had the personal experience of religion. It merely never occurred to him that all theological systems are but man-made rationalizations of order in the universe, and therefore worthy of only qualified veneration. Neither did it occur to him that he had in his own hand the key which would have let himself and all his brother ministers out of prison.

* * *

Since his death, the greatness of Jonathan Edwards has changed with the generations; inevitably so. As American life since 1758 has written itself afresh many times, new ideas and new modes of thinking them have reshaped the past as well as the present, postponing the final word. That at the distance of nearly two centuries what survives as his imprint upon the pattern of American culture bears little resemblance to what he put into the religious battles of his own time is also inevitable, and perhaps unimportant. His greatness as a religious leader, although it must have reference to both the timeliness and the permanence of his contribution, is strictly bounded by neither. What is his greatness? In a word, it is the greatness of one who had a determining part in initiating and directing a popular movement of far-reaching consequence, and who in addition, laid the foundations for a new system of religious thought, also of far-reaching consequence. Religious leaders have often directed popular movements. Less often they have founded systems of thought. Less often still has the same leader done both. This was, in part, the distinction of Jonathan Edwards. He was a compelling preacher and also a master logician and evangelist and also a thinker; a metaphysician on the side of the New Lights.

In both of these directions, his significance had chiefly to do with his emphasis on religion as a transforming individual experience, an emphasis he was privileged to make at one of the most favorable moments a religious leader could possibly have asked. His consequent success in what quickly became a great popular movement owed much to the hospitable time spirit, possibly more to the compulsion of his own personality and the force of his convictions; but it owed most of all to the idea itself, which really amounted to a redefinition of religion in terms of an inner, personal experience. By this new emphasis, which was really a much older emphasis, Jonathan Edwards became the initial, exciting force in a great religious crusade.

His mistake in choosing to speak through an outworn, dogmatic system instead of letting the new truth find more appropriate form of its own, was costly both to himself and to the truth he proclaimed. While he lived to speak directly, his ideas seemed more and the supporting framework less; but later, when he had gone and the traditional system

came to be recognized as obsolete, his ideas seemed obsolete also. Actually, he had made substantial changes in the modified Calvinism he professed; but he had made them by way of amendment only, substituting new elements for old, and keeping the traditional phraseology, even when he had changed the meaning behind it. What he did not see was that amendment was not enough. The whole theological system needed to be demolished, most of it thrown away, and the few remaining pieces used in the formulating of a quite new order. He had already gone a long way in this direction himself, possibly further than he knew, but not far enough to put him beyond the arid stretches of theological quibbling. The winning of many arguments became far too important. By his agility in dialectic he threw dust in the eyes of his brother intellectuals and also in his own. What he had to say did not require defence. It required only to be told. His failure to exchange a defensive warfare for leadership in a quite peaceful advance greatly limited his effectiveness in his own day. To a later judgment, it must also seriously qualify his greatness as an original thinker.

Considering the texture of his mind, one may wonder why he could not take the one more step and be free. Sometimes he did take it, but not habitually. He lacked the imagination; he lacked the mellowness and the flexibility which would have enabled him to get outside of the system and view it with enough detachment to judge it. He was on too narrow a track, and the surrounding walls were too high. For one whose thought was capable of telescopic range, and one who exhibited so large a degree of intellectual subtlety, his bondage seems almost a tragic pity. More than most men he was the prisoner of his own ideas. Yet this bondage presents no enigma. Back of it, in addition to the limitations of his personal heritage, lay three generations of Dissenting literalness, and far too many years of his own life spent in the far too industrious and too respectful study of pedestrian theologians, who trusted their hopes to logic and to logic alone. The vigor of Jonathan Edwards' moral earnestness has often enough been traced to the soil and the society from which he came. With equal reason one might say that his intellectual zeal and persistence and, in a measure, his intellectual blindness are traceable to the same sources. Among great Americans, he is perhaps the best example of one whose mind was cast strictly in the New England mold.

As an eighteenth century theologian, he was great in the scope and symmetry of his design. He saw the plan of redemption as a vast drama, stretching back to the fall of the angels and forward to the promise of just men made perfect in infinite ages beyond the last trump. Nothing was single; nothing was final; every end was merely a new beginning. His mind could not rest until he had brought the whole system within his ken, and unified it by a single idea.

Had he lived to complete the proposed "body of divinity," it might have borne little resemblance to the Edwardean scheme of theology as evolved by Messrs. Hopkins, Bellamy, Emmons, and their successors in another generation. These men were scarcely equal to their self-imposed task. Zealously they amassed proofs, filled in gaps, added argument to argument; but when all was finished they could not give the breath of life to what they had assembled. They had brought forth a system eminently useful for confronting point by point the system of their enemies, but one which had little

to offer a generation which needed not to be convinced so much as to be won back to a religious way of life. Men were tired of polemics. They needed a new challenge to belief, and it was already at hand. While the "New Divinity Gentlemen" had been busily amplifying, explaining, and neatly fitting part to part, the doctrines which their system was designed to confute had been quietly accepted by the larger portion of worshipping America. The great battle of argument, for which they were so excellently prepared, was never called. A chapter had ended, and there was no going back.

The impetus, however, which Jonathan Edwards had given to theological speculation is not to be judged by the ill success of the Edwardean scheme. Out of his own unfinished thought had come an intellectual movement which determined the main stream of religious debate for over a generation, and in its further sequel opened the way for the sectarian developments of the new century. To say that this same sectarianism is to be laid at his door is to credit one man with too much. For a hundred reasons, all roads led to separation in the church life of the mid-century, and no one man or group of men was responsible. Faint praise though it is, it would seem to be true that the attempt of a little coterie of friends, first to vindicate the master and later to modify his scheme in line with a more timely emphasis, was finally effective in the overthrow of the major tenets he had set himself to defend. The victory of the Arminian way of thought, as opposed to the Calvinistic, was perhaps inevitable in a post-Revolution America. God must be made more kind and man more worthy. But that the Edwardeans hastened the victory by their clarification of the doctrinal issues involved, and that by their intense zeal for a dying cause they forced men to declare their loyalties afresh, there can be little doubt. More ironically still, the triumphing idea as to the relation between this new kind of God and this new kind of man was once again the power of religion in the individual life. Under the very banner of his theological enemies Jonathan Edwards' concept of "heart religion" was still vital. It required only to be caught up by a new time spirit and shaped to answer to a new need. Looked back upon, the essential differences between his modifications of strict Calvinism and John Wesley's were slighter than might be supposed. John Wesley merely chose to make a different emphasis, and he proved to have made it in a fortunate hour. Methodism and the other evangelical sects made the experience of conversion once more a reality in the life of the average man, and thereby gave direction to the religious aspirations of another whole generation.

What has he for a later day? Exactly what he had for his own, once his thought is taken out of the theological idiom. What is the divine sovereignty, as a conviction to live by, but the hope of a world order that can be trusted? What is eternal punishment but the insistence that right must eventually triumph over wrong, if that world order be essentially stable and just? What is "election" but the recognition that there are those who can find God and those whom no amount of teaching and leading and compelling can ever bring to a desire even to search for Him? One cannot confer sight upon the blind. What is human depravity but the reluctant notion that, left to himself, man is no credit to his kind. Certain modern novelists have called it "realism" and have written screeds which make

Jonathan Edwards' view of original sin seem mild indeed.

Occasionally in his polemics and very often in his sermons, he laid by his theology and spoke his view of life directly. It is a pity he did not do it more often. If he had lived long enough to justify the ways of God to man in the whole panorama of the divine plan, and had then taken thought as to the essence of it all, he would have found in his hand a very simple thing. In the beginning it had been simple and in the end it would have been simple. Unfortunately he left it at a middle stage when specifications still seemed important. Fundamentally, his beliefs were the beliefs of the great religionists of all ages. He believed that man's life is of eternal consequence. He believed that the imperfect world we see cannot be all. He believed that reality is of the spirit. He believed that there is a pathway to present peace in spite of the frustrations of life, and that man can find it, but not of himself. Had he been able to clothe these ideas in images which would have stirred men's minds as the Enfield sermon stirred them, Emerson in his turn might have found other soil to plough.

As the details drop away, and his significance becomes clearer within the present century, the conclusion persists that as a shaping force in American culture, the man himself has been more important than anything he ever did or said or wrote. Among the great men of America, he is a lonely figure — perhaps the loneliest; and yet in spite of his severance from life as other men lived it, he stamped his personal imprint deep enough to outlast the generations. He was a man of one loyalty, and yet the total impression of his life, lived as it was without wide margins, or open spaces, or hearty human delights, is not an impression of narrowness or incompleteness. As an achievement in human living, the whole seems greater than the sum of its parts. Why, it is difficult to say, unless unity within the areas he knew helped to balance the realms he was content to let alone. By virtue of this same single-ness of loyalty, there was and is no mistaking what he stood for. Even while he lived, he became the bright symbol of what he called a thousand times and more, "the things of religion." It has been his peculiar triumph to make that identification permanent.

Peter Gay: THE OBSOLETE PURITANISM OF JONATHAN EDWARDS

Peter Gay is one of the foremost historical interpreters of the European Enlightenment. His recent study, The Enlightenment: An Interpretation *(1966) is significantly subtitled, "The Rise of Modern Paganism." In the light of his argument that the Enlightenment was a movement aimed at throwing off the repressive shackles of western Christendom, Gay believes that the habit of recent historians to exclaim over the extent and depth of Edwards' modernity requires considerable debunking. His study of Puritan historical thought includes an analysis of Edwards' sense of history. There are clear signs, Gay indicates, that in the final analysis Edwards was quite opposed to the progressive direction of the Enlightenment. Gay admits that Edwards was in many ways a most appealing and certainly significant colonial American, but that he remained a zealous advocate of a decayed and obsolete Puritanism far more medieval than modern.*

IN THE MIDST of the greatest revolution in the European mind since Christianity had overwhelmed paganism, Edwards serenely reaffirmed the faith of his fathers.

He had some notion that such a revolution was going on: he even read David Hume and professed himself "glad of an opportunity to read such corrupt books, especially when written by men of considerable genius"; it gave him, he said, "an idea of the notions that prevail in our nation." But he had no idea how extensive that revolution was, and how far his own historical thinking deviated from the historical thinking about to seize control of educated opinion in Europe. In fact, the nineteen years between Edwards' sermons and Edwards' death were decisive years in the rebellion of the Enlightenment against Christianity. Hume published the first two books of his *Treatise of Human Nature* in 1739; Condillac his *Essai sur l'origine des connaissances humaines* in 1746; Montesquieu his *Esprit des lois* in 1748, and with

From Peter Gay, *A Loss of Mastery: Puritan Historians in Colonial America* (Berkeley: University of California Press, 1966), pp. 91–94, 96–97, 104, 106–108, 113–116. Reprinted by permission of the University of California Press.

these books the foundations for the Enlightenment's epistemology, psychology, and sociology were firmly laid down. They were all attempts (in David Hume's words) "to introduce the experimental Method of Reasoning into Moral Subjects"; attempts to found the science of man on the ideas of Locke and the method of Newton. They were scientific rather than metaphysical, critical rather than credulous, naturalistic in temper, and wholly incompatible with revealed religion of any kind.

History, ready as always to follow the new currents, was beneficiary, and part, of the offensive of the secular against the Christian mind. In the late 1730's, while Edwards was displaying to his congregation the activity of Christ in history, Voltaire was at work on his *Siècle de Louis XIV,* a book which, with its anti-clericalism, its worldliness, and its aggressive modernity, became the manifesto, and the model, of the new history. A few years later, Voltaire began his vast *Essai sur les mœurs,* the Enlightenment's answer to Bossuet. Both of these books were published in Edwards' lifetime: the first in 1751, the second in 1756. Hume turned to historical subjects in the late 1740's; he started work on his *History of England* in 1752, and four years later published its first installment, covering the Stuart dynasty from the accession of James I to the expulsion of James II. William Robertson, the great Scottish historian whose reputation then was higher than it is now, began the first of his masterpieces, the *History of Scotland,* in 1753. Edward Gibbon, who combined the secular mentality of the *philosophes* with the technical competence of the *érudits,* was still a young man in those years, but he had already found his vocation, perfected his classical learning, and discovered his religious position; all he

needed was a subject commensurate with his talents, and he found that, with the lucid finality of a religious conversion, in 1764, only five years after Edwards' death.

To turn from these books to Edwards' *History of the Work of Redemption* is to leave the familiar terrain of the modern world with its recognizable features and legible signposts for a fantastic landscape, alive with mysterious echoes from a distant past, and intelligible only — if it can be made intelligible at all — with the aid of outmoded, almost primitive maps. The *philosophes'* histories made secular propaganda by providing information about a real past; Edwards' history made religious propaganda by arousing memories of a religious myth. To grasp the temper of Voltaire's or Hume's histories, one must read the new philosophy and collections of state papers; to grasp the temper of Edwards' history, one must read the Church Fathers and the Scriptures. However magnificent in conception, however bold in execution, Edwards' *History of the Work of Redemption* is a thoroughly traditional book, and the tradition is the tradition of Augustine.

* * *

For Edwards, secular history was on the whole insignificant, or significant only as it illustrated, illuminated, impinged upon sacred history: kings appear only as they establish, or obstruct, the true church, wars are mentioned only as they serve to spread, or to constrict, the true faith. All of parts one and two, and much of part three, of the *History of the Work of Redemption* consists of a free retelling of Scripture, with each miraculous event reported as a historical event. For Edwards, the authority of the Bible is absolute. "There were many great changes and revolutions in the world, and they were all only the turning of the wheels of Providence in order to this, to make way for the coming of Christ, and what he was to do in the world. They all pointed hither, and all issued here." Characters in the Old Testament acted in behalf of purposes greater than themselves, and prefigured great events of which they knew nothing, but they were real people, real historical subjects. There was an Adam and an Eve, and they sinned and awoke to their sense of guilt; there was a Cain and an Abel, a Noah and a Moses, and while they were symbols and types, they were symbols and types in the way all creaturely beings represent both themselves and God's intentions. In the modern sense, in the sense of Voltaire and Hume, almost none of Edwards' history is history — it is Calvinist doctrine exemplified in a distinct succession of transcendent moments.

* * *

If Edwards had been an ordinary Congregationalist pastor, his history would be remarkable only for its range and its style: its underlying philosophy offers no surprises. But Edwards was a brilliant scholar, a gifted student of science, a deft dialectician; he read as widely as Cotton Mather and to greater profit; he was open to the most abstruse and most advanced works of philosophy; he was among the first in the New England colonies to study Locke and appreciate Newton. His mind was the opposite of reactionary or fundamentalist. Yet his history was both. Such apparent contradictions are a sign of something extraordinary; with Jonathan Edwards, they are the mark of tragedy.

* * *

What made Edwards a tragic hero was this ruthlessly intelligent search for the meaning of Puritanism, pursued without regard to the cost. That terrible time in 1750, when his congregation dismissed him, was prefigured in all Edwards had thought and written since he entered Yale in 1716, a precocious young man of thirteen. From the beginning, he had loved God, and taken God's sovereignty seriously. He studied Newton and Locke, with hungry appetite, as he studied theology and apologetics, for the sake of God: "More convinced than ever of the usefulness of free, religious conversation," he wrote into his diary in 1724, deliberately merging an inferior with a superior sphere of inquiry. "I find by conversing on Natural Philosophy, that I gain knowledge abundantly faster, and see the reasons of things much more clearly than in private study: wherefore, earnestly to seek, at all times, for religious conversation." He was never the self-sufficient philosopher, always the strenuous servant of a higher power; he was aware, he wrote, that he was "unable to do anything without God." And, aware of that, he resolved with characteristic energy, "To endeavour to obtain for myself as much happiness, in the other world, as I possibly can, with all the power, might, vigour, and vehemence, yea violence, I am capable of, or can bring myself to exert, in any way that can be thought of." This devout violence marks all his work, even the most scholarly, and it led inescapably to that day, July 1, 1750, when Edwards preached his farewell sermon to a congregation that had voted to do without him — without *him*, Jonathan Edwards, the grandson and successor of Solomon Stoddard, who had for many years ruled western Massachusetts, they said, like a Protestant Pope.

It was an inescapable day because Jonathan Edwards insisted on rescuing the essence of the Puritan faith, on clarifying it, defending it, and preaching it to an age that did not wish to listen. Apologists for Edwards have made light of his most notorious performance, the Enfield sermon of 1741; at Enfield, Edwards had sent his hearers into fits of moaning, weeping, and lamentations by portraying man, with horrible specificity, as a sinner in the hands of an angry God, held over the flaming pit of hell by a thin thread, like a spider or other loathsome insect. It is true that this was not all of Edwards. He was as much the scholar and the polemicist as he was the fisher of souls. And often, he preached not hell fire for the damned but, with lyrical conviction, blissful peace for the saved. His doctrine of God satisfied his need to humble himself, to feel himself a vile worm before pure and ineffable Power, but it also satisfied his vigorous aesthetic appetite: his conviction of God's sovereignty, he said, was a "delightful conviction" which appeared to him "very often" as "exceeding pleasant, bright, and sweet." That, after all, as we know, was a central theme in his projected history of redemption: it would display God's design as "most beautiful and entertaining," musical in its "admirable contexture and harmony." All this is true. But to minimize the importance, and explain away the doctrine, of the Enfield sermon is to do Edwards a dubious favor; it is to make him inoffensive by emasculating him. Edwards did not want to be inoffensive. God was omnipotent, God was angry, man was wholly lost without God: these were the pillars sustaining the structure of Edwards' theology. To dissolve them into metaphors or disguise them with quibbles and qualifications would be to play Satan's game.

* * *

He was anything but an obscurantist, and, in his feverish intellectual excitement over the ideas of Newton and Locke, he sought to express the old religion in new ways. But the results were, as they had to be, pathetic: Jonathan Edwards philosophized in a cage that his fathers had built and that he unwittingly reinforced. The religious implications of Locke's sensationalist philosophy were inescapable, and they were drawn with surprising unanimity by Locke himself, by Locke's many followers, and by his detractors: revelation, to be true revelation, can be nothing more than an extension of reason; nearly all religious doctrine is either redundant or superstitious. For Locke, the only dogma a Christian need believe — the only dogma he can believe — is that Christ is the Messiah. But Edwards went right on accepting the testimony of Scriptures as literally true, accepting the predictions of the Apocalypse as authoritative history. He read Locke in careful isolation: Locke's psychology gave him useful material for understanding the quality of religious emotion, but little else.

Edwards' reading of Newton was equally parochial. It led him into some ingenious speculations about the nature of the physical universe and the future of mankind. Newton himself, it is true, was not a Newtonian all the time; unlike Locke, he left it to others to explicate, and to complete, his system; unlike Locke, he found pleasure in delving into Biblical chronology and chiliastic prophecies. But, whatever Newton's private religious explorations — and they remain a matter of heated controversy — the ultimate religious direction of Newton's system was away from fundamentalism, away from chiliasm — away, in a word, from Puritanism — toward rationalism, Unitarianism, simple Theism. The physical universe of Edwards was not the physical universe of Newton: it was a universe created in six days, filled with angels and devils, with a heaven and a hell, a universe in the hands, and at the mercy, of an angry God. Edwards did not become a Puritan, or remain a Puritan, as a result of his philosophical and scientific inquiries; he exploited modern ideas and modern rhetoric to confirm religious convictions he had held all his life, and accepted on other grounds.

The complete incompatibility of Edwards' system of ideas with the new world of enlightened philosophy has been obscured by Edwards' vocabulary. It is not that he adopted modish words for modish purposes; but he delighted in intellectual investigation, his ear was sensitive, and his curiosity acute. Hence he felt the power of the new imagery and the new language, and freely used them in his writings. He appealed to "history, observation, and experience," and claimed, as a good empiricist, to bow to fact. But the history he cited was the infallible Scriptures; the observations he noted are the observations of Biblical characters or contemporary Christians in a state of religious trance; the experience

he valued was the revelation that gives man knowledge of God. Edwards' facts are of the same order. The *Essay Concerning Human Understanding* and the *Principia Mathematica* may have been important to him, the Pentateuch and the book of Revelation were indispensable. "A great Divine," Ezra Stiles justly called Edwards, "a good linguist" and "a good Scholar," thoroughly versed in "the Logic of Ramus and Burgersdisius, & the philosophy of Wendeline," but not in "the Mathematics & the Ratiocina of the Newtonian Philosophy."

Edwards' spiritual isolation was exacerbated by his physical isolation. In Europe, the ideas of Newton and Locke called forth vigorous debate; they were tested and extended. The followers of Newton and Locke, goaded by their critics, gradually constructed an enlightened intellectual system of great power and lasting influence. Edwards had no such advantages; when he corresponded with Europeans, it was mainly with like-minded clerics; when he read — and he read deeply and voraciously — he read mainly books that would feed his Puritan convictions, or books that he thought he needed to refute. The outside world existed mainly to supply him with echoes. Far from being the first modern American, therefore, he was the last medieval American — at least among the intellectuals.

Conrad Cherry: EDWARDS NEITHER MEDIEVAL NOR MODERN

Conrad Cherry of Pennsylvania State University makes extensive use of recent interpretations in his reappraisal of Edwards' thought and its place in the history of ideas. Cherry is critical of the trend to transport Edwards into the twentieth century, but he does not believe Edwards' religious orientation makes him useless in understanding the modern American temper, as others have indicated. Cherry argues that Edwards was devoted to traditional religious questions still essential to his era, and answered them within the framework of a still acceptable Augustinian, Calvinistic and Puritan piety. His originality lay in his acceptance of the challenge which eighteenth-century rationalism put to orthodoxy, and his use of Enlightenment thought to answer its own challenge. Cherry suggests this is evident in Edwards' loyal defense of religious experience against Arminian attacks. Cherry concludes that, on these grounds, Edwards reconciled the conflicting movements of the era more successfully than any other colonial intellectual.

TOWARD THE END of the last century Jonathan Edwards was examined psychologically and was judged a fanatic who expounded unpalatable Calvinist doctrines adopted in a "period of religious delirium." The picture of Edwards as a curious, rather mad, eighteenth-century preacher preoccupied with hell-fire, a God of wrath, and the hatred of "all of Adam's children with a hatred bordering on the pathological" is an image that is still with us. It is clearly embodied in Phyllis McGinley's little rendition of the God of Edwards:

> Abraham's God, the Wrathful One,
>   Intolerant of error —
> Not God the Father or the Son
>   But God the Holy Terror.

Images have a way of fixing themselves in the American consciousness, and this image of Edwards is not easily shattered. But recent reappraisals of the life and thought of Jonathan Edwards have performed a significant measure of iconoclasm in the process of attaining a more accurate view of the man and his times. It is becoming apparent that the caricatures of Edwards as a hater of men, a hell-fire preacher, a worshiper of a wrathful God usually arise from a very limited acquaintance with Edwards' works or from a Procrustean attitude toward figures of the past. We have been wisely warned that too often Edwards' famous Enfield sermon, "Sinners in the Hands of an Angry God," has been taken as the model of Edwards' preaching without balancing it with his other sermons or, sometimes, without a very careful study of the symbols and the intention of that sermon itself. Even more productive of the Edwards caricatures has been the temptation to treat as so much nonsense — or at best, as comic quaintness — whatever cannot be adjusted to some nineteenth- or twentieth-century world view. Clyde Holbrook has directed us to the fact that the caricatures are as much a commentary on the interpreters of Edwards as on Edwards himself. The tendency has been to paint Edwards as a religious fanatic because his sense of man's tragedy and eternal destiny "before a majestic and holy God whose purposes are not identifiable with ours" is at odds with his detractors' theological assumptions that tame God "to the point where he can will or execute nothing which would offend a cultured Westerner."

Certainly a part of the breakthrough to a fresh understanding of Edwards is owing to the renaissance in Puritan studies in our century. Historical, literary, philosophical, and theological approaches to the Puritans of New England have been setting aside old stereotypes in order to get an unbiased picture of early American life and letters. Not only has this meant a greater appreciation of the historical context of Puritan New England, of the peculiar problems and challenges facing seventeenth- and eighteenth-century Puritans; it has also meant the recognition that contemporary American traits are linked with New England Puritanism — traits other than those associated with our historically misleading term "puritanical." The mingling of the sense of national destiny with religious zeal and purpose, for example, has a complicated history in this country; but it certainly found an impetus in the Puritan effort to set up in the New World a political-religious "City upon a Hill" for all the world to behold. To the degree that new approaches to Puritanism correct what Edmund S. Morgan has rightly judged a common tendency — attributing "whatever is wrong with the American mind . . . to its Puritan ancestry" and smothering the remainder of Puritanism "under a homespun mantle of quaintness" — the picture of Edwards, himself

an heir and proponent of Puritanism, is also corrected.

Nevertheless, even when the stereotyped images are abandoned, interpreters of Edwards still feel uncomfortable with Edwards' Calvinism. To alleviate the pain of embarrassment, features of Edwards' thought are frequently searched out which "transcend" his Calvinism or which prefigure the post-Puritan era of American thought. Perhaps such a procedure would not be totally inappropriate if Edwards had not so obviously addressed himself to problems current in his eighteenth century or if he had not consciously chosen Puritan Calvinism as the framework for so much of his thought. One therefore suspects a ghost of the perspective yielding the older caricatures in a recent study of Edwards, which proceeds on the assumption that it is at the points where Edwards departs from main-line Puritan theology "that the present-day student has most to learn from America's most neglected theologian." And Perry Miller, to whom every contemporary student of Edwards and the Puritans is profoundly indebted, leads one to conclude that Edwards is to be appreciated primarily at points other than where traditional Calvinist tenets receive extensive treatment. In his brilliant portrayal of Edwards as an American precursor of modern epistemology and physical theory, Miller frequently minimizes themes of Calvinist thought which were at the forefront of Edwards' reflective concerns.

For good or for ill, Edwards was a Calvinist theologian; and, as a Calvinist theologian, he claimed the heritage of his New England forefathers. Edwards did request his readers not to refer to him as a "Calvinist" if they meant that he was dependent on every feature of Calvin's own thought or that he held certain doctrines because Calvin "believed and taught them," and there is evidence that his Puritan tradition drew as much, if not more, from the Rhineland reformers as from Calvin. Yet Edwards was willing "to be called a Calvinist, for distinction's sake," and his thought was pervaded by the same visions that had caught the imagination of both Calvin and the Puritans: the sovereignty and freedom of God; the drama of history as the story both of man's tragic fallenness and of God's renewed purpose to deliver; man's frailty and unworthiness in comparison with the justice and mercy of a majestic God; the personal and social value of a disciplined, "holy" life of "practice." And though Edwards would have resisted having his thought reduced to that of his Puritan predecessors, he would have also insisted that if one learned from him *only* at the points where he departed from their thought, then one would not really learn from him at all. It was no thoughtless appeal to tradition when, on the occasion of the death of his influential uncle, Col. John Stoddard, Edwards praised Stoddard as a "strong rod of the community" because he "was thoroughly established in those religious principles and doctrines of the first fathers of New England."

To be sure, Edwards was no slave to his theological heritage. . . . He was critical of many aspects of his Puritan tradition, and he held that it was a thinker's task in each generation to bring new light to bear upon perennial concerns. In the preface to a book by his friend and former student, Joseph Bellamy, Edwards discourages the theologian "in an obscure part of the world" from taking refuge in formulations of the past:

They . . . who bring any addition of light

to this great subject, *The nature of true religion,* and its distinction from all counterfeits, should be accepted as doing the greatest possible service to the Church of God. And attempts to this end ought not to be despised and discouraged, under a notion that it is but vanity and arrogance in such as are lately sprung up in an obscure part of the world, to pretend to add anything on this subject, to the informations we have long since received from their fathers, who have lived in former times, in *New England,* and more noted countries. We cannot suppose that the Church of God is already possessed of all that light, in things of this nature, that ever God intends to give it; nor that all Satan's lurking-places have already been found out.

Furthermore, Edwards' intellectual interests were broad for a man of frontier America. Although he complained that he was not "better informed what books there are, that are published on the other side of the Atlantic," he eagerly accepted what books friends could send him from abroad. His "Catalogue" of books reveals a reading interest in philosophy, science, mathematics, and literature as well as theology; and he continued to borrow from the various disciplines in his reflections. It is now patent fact that he turned to his own design the insights of such thinkers as John Locke, Francis Hutcheson and the Cambridge Platonists. But the interests which occupied Edwards' chief attention were theological — interests which increasingly had their immediate occasions in the theological issues facing eighteenth-century New England. His philosophical and scientific interests were bent to a theological purpose. Edwards chose to broaden, impregnate and somtimes alter his Calvinist theology, rather than transcend it. And Edwards' Puritan ancestors would themselves have delighted in Edwards' efforts to feed new life into theology with the broadest possible learning. Daniel Boorstin illustrates a difference between Quaker and Puritan attitudes toward "worldly knowledge" with the story of the Quaker who in the 1750s patronized the shop of a studious barber. The barber once displayed proudly a book in algebra which he had been studying. The Quaker records that his reply to the barber was: "I said it might be useful to some, but that I could take up grubbing, or follow the plough, without studying algebra; as he might also shave a man, etc. without it. Besides I found it a more profitable and delightful study, to be quietly employed in learning the law of the Lord written in mine own heart, so that I might walk before him acceptably." Boorstin comments that in contrast to the Quaker's sanctimonious remark, in the same situation "a Puritan might have admired the barber's industry, have expressed interest in his subject, and finally perhaps have noted that God himself was the greatest of all algebraists." For Edwards, as for his forefathers, most any subject could be studied to the glory of God; and to the degree that such subjects could strengthen the appeal of the great themes of Calvinist theology, they were bent to that purpose.

There is, of course, no guarantee that Jonathan Edwards' century and conceptual framework will not be received as just so many "dead husks" by us in the twentieth century. History has a way of denying us such guarantees. There are, for example, historical factors which may well stop our ears to any real hearing of Edwards' Calvinism. In doing battle with its theological and philosophical foes (notably Deistic rationalism), Calvinist orthodoxy hardened its traditional doctrines into static, revealed truths, rational consent to which was made tanta-

mount to religious faith even if that involved a *sacrificium intellectus*. This was a far cry from Edwards' own understanding of the doctrines as living symbols of a living faith, but those who are heirs of this petrifying process tend to hear Edwards through it. There are many such factors in American religious history which unpleasantly filter Edwards' words. Yet we are possessed of abilities and forces that may *at least* make us aware of the filters and *at best* free us for authentic understanding. For one thing, we are quite simply capable of bringing our past under examination — of inquiring into how our political, social and religious ideals and faiths have been shaped by our past; and which aspects of our history have been deleterious, and which beneficial, for our present and future self-understanding. A leap completely out of our own contemporary skins is both impossible and undesirable; but a degree of historical self-transcendence *is* possible and is able to deliver the meaning and relevance of Edwards' thought and century. Furthermore, we have witnessed a phenomenon on the twentieth-century intellectual scene which has shed new — or at least, neglected — light upon Calvinism. The leading doctrines of the Calvinist tradition have been reinterpreted as symbols laden with meaning relevant to the contemporary situation. Whatever quarrel one may have with specific features of the theologies of such thinkers as Karl Barth and Reinhold Niebuhr, they have, in diverse ways, reclaimed Augustinian and Calvinist categories in order to prick the contemporary conscience, wean man away from religious sentimentality, and throw him up against the hard reality of a God who judges as well as forgives. This has meant a calling into question: Western man's all-too-easy conscience;

his sometimes hidden belief that he can, through the manipulation of his world and others, manipulate his ultimate destiny; his identification of his humanitarian feelings with righteousness, which amounts to a glorious façade for unrighteousness and injustice. And it has meant that the doctrine of original sin points once again to man's drive to deify himself and his own private systems, that the doctrine of free and "irresistible" grace represents man's inability to fulfill the demands of his essential being and his need of an unearned gift of freedom and meaning from beyond himself, that the once deplorable doctrine of predestination symbolizes man's precarious situation in the presence of a God whose will cannot be reduced to our purposes.

Suggestions for Additional Reading

A number of volumes in American intellectual history will enable the reader to probe further into the topic of the relationship between Jonathan Edwards and the Enlightenment. Stow Persons, *American Minds* (New York, 1958) has several excellent interpretative chapters on colonial religion and the Enlightenment. A number of Perry Miller's articles revolutionized current views of colonial Puritanism and the Great Awakening. Fortunately, they have been collected in *Errand Into the Wilderness* (Cambridge, Mass., 1956) and are indispensable for further understanding of the issues in the eighteenth century. While it asks fewer probing questions, Merle Curti, *The Growth of American Thought* (3rd ed., New York, 1966) includes chapters on colonial religion and the Age of Reason which are unsurpassed in their encyclopedic detail. There is a brief treatment of Edwards as a powerful reactionary in Max Savelle, *Seeds of Liberty: The Genesis of the American Mind* (New York, 1948). Herbert W. Schneider's *A History of American Philosophy* (2nd ed., New York, 1963) places Edwards in the broad perspective of the history of Platonism and idealism, and Vincent Buranelli, "Colonial Philosophy," *William and Mary Quarterly*, (third series), XVI (July, 1959), 343–362 reviews both the history of colonial philosophy and the several interpretations of Edwards. Points of view on Edwards are also excellently considered in Clyde A. Holbrook, "Jonathan Edwards and His Detractors," *Theology Today*, X (October, 1963), 384–396, while R. R. Stearn's article, "Assessing the New England Mind," *Church History*, X (September, 1941), 246–262 is helpful in exploring

revised interpretations of all of Puritanism. C. H. Faust, "The Decline of Puritanism," in *Transitions in American Literary History*, ed. by H. H. Clark (Durham, N. C., 1953) looks at Edwards' position as an attempt to delay the decline of Puritanism in the eighteenth century. One of the most original volumes in recent years, Alan Heimert's *Religion and the American Mind* (Cambridge, Mass., 1967), forcefully suggests that Calvinism of the Edwardean strain played a far greater role than usually suspected in the development of an American culture, and indeed did more to bring about the American Revolution than liberal enlightened rationalism.

Important studies of the Enlightenment itself should not be ignored, since its American phase was so largely dependent upon European and British developments. Sir Leslie Stephen's *History of English Thought in the Eighteenth Century*, (2 vols., New York, 1876, 1902, 1962) is old but has not been superseded in its comprehensive detail, and specific materials on Edwards' English opposition are available in Ronald N. Stromberg, *Religious Liberalism in Eighteenth Century England* (New York, 1954). Other important and complementary studies are Ernst Cassirer, *The Philosophy of the Enlightenment* (Princeton, 1951); Carl L. Becker, *The Heavenly City of the Eighteenth Century Philosophers* (New Haven, 1932); and Peter Gay, *The Enlightenment* (New York, 1967). Two articles by Alfred O. Aldridge relate Edwards and individual English philosophers: "Jonathan Edwards and William Godwin on Virtue," *American Literature*, XVIII (January, 1947), 308–318, and "Edwards and

Hutcheson," *Harvard Theological Review*, XLIV (January, 1951), 35–53. There is also an article, "Edwards and Newton," *Philosophical Review*, XLIX (November, 1940), 609–622, by James H. Tufts.

The best volume of readings on Edwards, with an admirable introduction, is C. H. Faust and T. H. Johnson, *Jonathan Edwards: Representative Selections* (rev. ed., New York, 1962). The first completely new edition of all of Edwards' works in over a century, with modern editing, was initiated by the Yale University Press, with the late Perry Miller as its general editor. Unfortunately, only two volumes have so far been published, both with comprehensive introductions: *Freedom of the Will*, ed. by Paul Ramsey (1957), and *Religious Affections*, ed. by John E. Smith (1959). Many of the older editions, however, are quite excellent. Interested readers will also want to read reconstructions of Edwards' own personal notes in Harvey G. Townsend, ed., *The Philosophy of Jonathan Edwards From His Private Notebooks* (Eugene, Oregon, 1955), and Leon Howard, ed., *"The Mind" of Jonathan Edwards: A Reconstructed Text* (Berkeley, 1963). Thomas H. Johnson's "Jonathan Edwards' Background of Reading," *Publications of the Colonial Society of Massachusetts*, XXVIII (December, 1931), 193–222 covers a critical topic to determine the influence of the Enlightenment upon Edwards. Perry Miller also edited a volume of Edwards' manuscripts, *Images or Shadows of Divine Things* (New Haven, 1948), which led Miller to call Edwards "the first American empiricist."

A number of important biographies of Edwards have also found their way into print, beginning with Sereno Edwards Dwight, *The Life of President Edwards* (New York, 1830), which contains details and documents otherwise unavailable. Solid and sympathetic biographies, with useful information, are A. V. G. Allen, *Jonathan Edwards* (Boston, 1889), and A. C. McGiffert, *Jonathan Edwards* (New York, 1932), while Henry Bamford Parkes, *Jonathan Edwards: The Fiery Puritan* (New York, 1930) is unsympathetic. More recent is A. O. Aldridge, *Jonathan Edwards* (New York, 1964). Perhaps the best brief account is Francis A. Christie, "Jonathan Edwards," *Dictionary of American Biography*, VI, 30–37. A number of intellectual biographies have also appeared, including Edward H. Davidson, *Jonathan Edwards: The Narrative of a Puritan Mind* (Boston, 1966), a study which follows Miller's train of thought. Douglas J. Elwood, *The Philosophical Theology of Jonathan Edwards* (New York, 1960) looks at Edwards as a forerunner of modern existentialism, who anticipated many of the dilemmas of modern man. The reader ought also to consider G. P. Fisher, "The Philosophy of Jonathan Edwards," *North American Review*, CXXXVIII (March, 1879), 284–303; E. G. Smyth, "Jonathan Edwards' Idealism," *American Journal of Theology*, I (October, 1897), 950–964; and H. N. Gardiner, "The Early Idealism of Jonathan Edwards," *Philosophical Review* IX (November, 1900), 673–696. Two articles by Rufus Suter look at Edwards as a physical scientist: "An American Pascal: Jonathan Edwards," *Scientific Monthly*, LXVIII (May, 1949), 338–342, and "The Strange Universe of Jonathan Edwards," *Harvard Theological Review*, LIV (April, 1961), 125–128. J. McK. Cattell, "Jonathan Edwards on Multidimensional Space and the Mechanistic Concept of Life," *Science* LII (October 29, 1920), 409–410 says Edwards anticipated Einstein. Perhaps the most satisfactory look at the contribution of Edwards to the development of American psychology is in J. W. Fay, *American Psychology before William James* (New Brunswick, N.J., 1939). See also E. E. Slosson, "Jonathan Edwards as a Freudian," *Science,* new series, LII (December 24, 1920), 609. Other specialized articles include H. G. Townsend, "The Will and the Understanding in the Philosophy of Jonathan Edwards," *Church History* XVI (December, 1940), 210–220; A. E. Murphy, "Jonathan Edwards on Free Will and Moral Agency," *Philosophical Review,* LXVIII (May, 1959), 181–202; and James Orr, "Jonathan Edwards: His Influence in Scotland," *Congregationalist and Christian World,* LXXXVIII (October 3, 467–469).

While this volume dwelt upon Edwards' relationship to the Enlightenment, he was also the single most important revivalist and theologian in American religious history. Edwards' role in the Great Awakening is covered at length by Joseph Tracy, *The Great Awakening* (New York, 1845), and Edwin S. Gaustad, *The Great Awakening in New England* (New York, 1957). Frank H. Foster, *A Genetic History of the New England Theology* (Chicago, 1909), and Joseph Haroutunian, *Piety Versus Moralism: The Passing of the New England Theology* (New York, 1932) are both superb studies of Edwards' domination of the American theological scene. The reader should also consult H. Shelton Smith, *Changing Conceptions of Original Sin: A Study in American Theology Since 1750* (New York, 1955). The best study of Charles Chauncy is in Conrad Wright, *The Beginnings of Unitarianism in America* (Boston, 1955), and G. A. Koch, *Republican Religion: The American Revolution and the Cult of Reason* (New York, 1933) describes the spread of liberal religion so abhorrent to Edwards.